# The Future of
# Western Development Assistance

# About the Book and Authors

Since the inception of Western development assistance, significant changes in the makeup of donors, recipients, development goals, and strategies have taken place. However, major donor institutions have not yet weighed the impact of these changes on their operations and objectives in anticipation of the future global environment.

Discussing trends that will profoundly affect development assistance strategy, the authors raise such questions as: Will the demand for Western technical assistance drop sharply over the next decade? Was the Latin American debt crisis precipitated by the loan practices of international commercial banks? Should aid to Africa be shifted from investment in rural desert areas to investment in urban planning and infrastructure? Also examined are such concerns as the outside management of agricultural research; the U.S. focus on purchasing political allegiance with its aid programs, thus creating dependent nations; the threat to East Asian economic growth posed by the micro-electronics revolution; and the growing conflict between western aid and trade objectives. The authors' purpose is not to provide definitive prescriptions for future development programs, but rather to focus the attention of policymakers on important, but often neglected, issues.

Elliott R. Morss is associate director of the Center for Asian Development Studies and adjunct professor of economics, Boston University. Victoria A. Morss is a consultant for a number of bilateral and multilateral donor agencies.

# The Future of
# Western Development Assistance

Elliott R. Morss
Victoria A. Morss

Westview Press / Boulder and London

88/TO22767

*Westview Special Studies in Social, Political, and Economic Development*

-------------------------------------------------------------------------
This Westview softcover edition was manufactured on our own premises using
equipment and methods that allow us to keep even specialized books in stock.
It is printed on acid-free paper and bound in softcovers that carry the
highest rating of the National Association of State Textbook Administrators,
in consultation with the Association of American Publishers and the Book
Manufacturers' Institute.
-------------------------------------------------------------------------

Published in 1986 in the United States of America by Westview Press, Inc.;
Frederick A. Praeger, Publisher; 5500 Central Avenue, Boulder, Colorado 80301

Library of Congress Cataloging-in-Publication Data
Morss, Elliott R.
   The future of Western development assistance.
   (Westview special studies in social, political, and
economic development)
   Includes index.
   1. Economic development.  2. Economic assistance--
Developing countries.  I. Morss, Victoria A.  II. Title.
III. Series.
HD75.M67  1986        338.9           86-15824
ISBN 0-8133-7269-0

HD
75
.M67
1986

Composition for this book was provided by the authors.
This book was produced without formal editing by the publisher.

Printed and bound in the United States of America

 The paper used in this publication meets the requirements of the
American National Standard for Permanence of Paper for Printed
Library Materials Z39.48-1984.

6    5    4    3    2    1

# Contents

# Tables

# Preface

For most of history man has attempted to explain events, attributing actions to causes, linking together patterns to form an understandable picture. Societal change has been studied from the perspective of many disciplines; progress has been measured and judged according to varied interpretations of countless traditions, prosaic facts, and even myths. Mathematical reasoning has confronted passionate humanitarian appeals. Rational views of the world verified by theories of religion, philosophy, history, politics, ethics, and science have been challenged by bitter, real social conflicts and cultural problems. Nowhere has the conflict between the desire to achieve modernity while providing for all humanitarian needs been greater than in the developing world today.

The primary aim of this book is to document some of the changes in world conditions that lead one to wonder about the appropriateness of current western development activities. From such a starting point one could go in a number of different directions. To avoid confusion we state our premises at the outset. The development process is based on predictions: if certain actions are taken in a particular environment a complex chain of events will be set in motion resulting in anticipated changes. In fact, that rarely happens. The process of change is not that scientific; it is really a subtle mixture of analysis and advocacy, fraught with uncertainty, ignorance, and risks. The chance of success is remote, requires rigorous persistence, an intense desire to accomplish something, and most importantly, a better historical understanding of global dynamics.

xii

As in many professions, the tendency in the
development field is to want immediate solutions to
problems, to look for a quick, technical answer and to
forget the evolution of ideas and events that led to where
we are today.  But successful policy makers recognize
their decisions and choices are based on political issues,
legal, bureaucratic, procedural problems, and cultural
achievements and aspiration that started long ago and will
continue years into the future.[1] To raise some of the
issues that are too frequently overlooked by decision
makers, to ask some different questions, and redefine the
nature of the development problem is our objective.  We do
not have simple answers, or pretend that the issues raised
are immutable. But here are our assumptions about the
nature of the development process:

1. The primary rationale for western development
   assistance is to equip developing nations with
   the willingness and capacity to function
   effectively in a world dominated by western
   norms, values, and processes.

2. Ultimately, nations will aspire for the freedom
   to chart their own future.  This means efforts
   to purchase their political and economic
   allegiance will be resented and fail.

3. It is not in the interest of western nations to
   accede to the demands of developing nations to
   influence a major redistribution of global
   resources.

4. Economic assistance should not serve to prop up
   governments unable or unwilling to adopt
   measures that fundamentally affect their
   development progress.

5. Countries reach a point where their aggregate
   development is sufficiently advanced to warrant
   a cessation of foreign aid even though pockets
   of poverty remain.

A few of our development colleagues, busy as they
are in serving the immediate needs of the development
industry, have shown interest in this book.  We greatly
appreciate the curiosity and encouragement provided at
various times by Richard Blue, Neva Goodwin, Oliver
Oldman, Alexander Shakow, and Paul Streeten.  We are
particularly indebted to Gus Papanek, director of the
Center for Asian Studies at Boston University, and to

David Brown and Jane Covey of the Institute of Development
Research for providing institutional settings in which
this book was completed.

*Elliott R. Morss*
*Victoria A. Morss*

NOTES

[1]  Some of the problems that can result when policy makers
do not have a sufficient historical perspective are
documented by Richard E. Neustadt and Ernest R. May,
Thinking in Time (New York: The Free Press, 1986).

# 1

## The Changing Circumstances of Developed Nations

The economic and political conditions that led the United States to initiate large-scale foreign assistance efforts following World War II no longer exist.[1] A significant portion of the productive capacity of Western Europe and Japan had been destroyed and their economies were near collapse. The Soviet Union was reeling from the loss of 20 million people and its economy was in total disarray. Survival was a challenge for many nations: mass starvation was seen as a real possibility, medical facilities were inadequate, and unemployment was rampant. As a poignant indicator of how desperate conditions had become one observer has suggested that the infant mortality rate in Germany then was higher than it is today in Sahelian Africa.[2]

The United States was then in a position of complete economic dominance. Today it is hard to imagine the extent of this dominance. Until well into the 1960s, a serious debate took place among leading international economists over whether or not the U.S. would always have a surplus balance of trade that would exert a deflationary impact on the rest of the world.[3] Consider that in 1960, U.S. corporations had about 25 percent of the world market share in manufacturing, and controlled 95 percent of the domestic market for automobiles, steel, and consumer electronics.[4]

Following World War II, Congress and government officials believed it was essential to create an environment in which earlier failures were not repeated. The belief was that unless the United States used its economic resources to help its allies and enemies revive their economies they would not be able to support the growth of a healthy world economy based on the principles

1

of free trade, convertibility, normal international capital flows, and democratic processes. Greater productivity was seen as the key to peace and prosperity. It was argued that without assistance from the United States, these nations might resort to nondemocratic or communist solutions to their problems. Moreover, as Stalin's intentions became clear in 1947, the potential loss of Europe to a hostile power was considered a direct security threat to the United States. And from a national perspective, policy makers were concerned the postwar period would be accompanied by considerable unemployment in the United States. Building the economies in Europe would create markets for American products, which in turn would create jobs and ease the transition from a war-time to a peace-time economy. In short, the first assistance program was based on a combination of humanitarian concerns to reduce human suffering and misery, economic self-interest, and a conviction that economic growth was a prerequisite for peace and spread of democracy.[5]

As economic recovery in Europe gained momentum and the military situation stabilized, a new notion evolved to the effect that a modified assistance effort directed at the less fortunate nations in Latin America, Asia, Africa, and the Middle East might generate similar economic growth. This, it was thought, would lead to widespread adoption of capitalist practices and allegiance to the United States and democratic principles. Also, a growing resentment was being articulated in the councils of the United Nations that the enormous amount of assistance the United States provided to Europe, which had a relatively decent standard of living, was unjust so long as millions of people in the Third World "languished in extreme poverty." In response to these conditions President Truman articulated in his inaugural address of January 1949 a new, modest program to assist the peoples in the developing world. He said: "I believe that we should make available to peace-loving peoples the benefits of our store of technical knowledge in order to help them realize their aspirations for a better life. ...Democracy alone can supply the vitalizing force to stir the peoples of the world into triumphant action...."[6]

Government policy makers regarded an expanded assistance program to the Third World in a positive light and the corporate sector shared their perspective. Aid disbursements would ease worldwide dollar shortages and create demand for American products. As one international observer pointed out: "...the interests of the U.S.

economy coincided with a system that promoted world welfare."[7]

After the Korean war, the character of the assistance program to developing nations changed. It was no longer a purely economic assistance program to foster long-term development. Now the focus was on military assistance to limit communist aggression. This is not to say that the foreign assistance program was ever seen in any other light than as an instrument of U.S. foreign policy; but as global circumstances changed, the emphasis of the program altered to meet national foreign policy objectives.

In passing, it is important to remember that these international assistance programs were developed by government officials and their advisors. The programs were announced to a largely indifferent American public that was primarily concerned with seeing its country disengage from international activities and the return of the troops.

CONDITIONS TODAY IN THE UNITED STATES

Today circumstances are different. The United States has lost its position of total economic dominance; it is now one of a number of economically strong countries. Western Europe rebuilt its productive capacity; Japan and other countries in Asia developed strong technical capabilities to compete with U.S. industries; a number of African nations went through a transition from colonialism to independence; Latin American countries developed strong, multidimensional economies and the Arab oil embargo in 1973-1974 exposed the economic vulnerability of all industrialized nations. By 1979 the U.S. share of world manufactured goods had slipped to just 17 percent. Between 1972 and 1978 industrial production grew at a rate of 4 percent per year in West Germany and over 5 percent annually in Japan. In stark contrast, it grew at only 1 percent per annum in the United States, and U.S. control over its domestic market eroded. Less than 50 percent of electronic consumer products sold in the United States in 1979 were produced in America.[8] In 1986 the United States is confronted by a staggering, non-sustainable trade deficit, while Japan has built up a large trade surplus. In a sentence: the rest of the world is catching up with the United States.

This change in relative economic power raises two basic questions:

1. Is it reasonable for the citizens of the United States and other western nations to support the provision of economic assistance to countries that are developing industries that displace western workers?

2. From the standpoint of global economic equilibrium, should the United States be expected to bear such a large share of the foreign assistance burden?

Regarding the first question, economists repeatedly make the point that foreign aid, by contributing to economic growth, is creating markets for western products. Indeed, this argument was an essential justification of the Marshall Plan. One need not question the validity of this assertion to recognize it will not satisfy western workers who lose their jobs because of lower-cost imports. At the very least, this argument is not likely to be as politically effective as it was ten or fifteen years ago when production from developing countries was not seen as displacing western industry.

As to the second question, it is reasonable to argue that as the economic status of nations change, there should be mechanisms to change their relative contributions of development assistance. And while the international development community has established criteria for country contributions of official development assistance (ODA), the system works imperfectly. Country contributions to ODA tend to fluctuate with changes in domestic economic circumstances and political winds. And further, there is reason to question the appropriateness of the criteria employed.[9]

CHANGING ASSISTANCE LEVELS AND DONOR SHARES

The magnitude of ODA has increased substantially since World War II, as have the number of donor countries and multilateral organizations providing economic assistance to developing countries. As table 1.1 shows, the net official development assistance in 1970 was $8.4 billion. By 1980 it had grown to $40 billion. For the past ten years the average rate of increase in net disbursements of ODA has been more than 4 percent per year, measured in constant prices and exchange rates.[10]

Table 1.1
Net ODA by Donor Group[a], 1970-1982
(In real $ billions)

| Group | 1970 | 1975 | 1980 | 1982 |
|---|---|---|---|---|
| OECD Countries | 6.95 | 13.85 | 27.26 | 27.73 |
| OPEC Countries | 0.40 | 6.24 | 9.59 | 5.89 |
| CMEA[b] and Other Countries | 1.00 | 1.99 | 3.10 | 3.33 |
| TOTAL | 8.35 | 22.08 | 39.95 | 36.90 |

Source: OECD, Development Co-operation 1984 Review, p. 64.
[a] This includes bilateral aid and contributions to
multilateral donor agencies.
[b] Council for Mutual Economic Assistance (Eastern Bloc
countries) and all other donors.

Historically, the seventeen countries in the
Organization for Economic Co-operation and Development
(OECD) have contributed one-half to two-thirds of all
official development assistance distributed to developing
nations. However, their goal of contributing 0.7 percent
of gross national product (GNP) has never been reached as
a group. In 1970 official development assistance amounted
only 0.35 percent of of their combined GNP. By 1982 that
percentage had increased slightly to 0.38 percent of GNP,
but still only just over half of the targeted amount.[11]
Until the 1973-1974 increase in oil prices, few OPEC
members provided significant economic assistance. In 1970
their total contribution to official flows was $40
million, or 5 percent of ODA. After the escalation of oil
prices, the level of assistance from OPEC countries
increased dramatically. By 1980 they contributed 16
percent of ODA, or $9 billion. Since then their
contribution has declined by over 40 percent, reflecting a
reduction in oil revenues and political conflicts. Still,
OPEC nations on average give a much larger percentage of
GNP than do OECD donors. As a percent of total GNP,
official flows from OPEC nations reached 8.5 percent in
1975; it then dropped to 2.7 percent in 1982.[12]
The official flows provided by the Council for Mutual
Economic Assistance (CMEA) and other countries increased
threefold from $1 billion in 1970 to $3.3 billion in 1982.
It is estimated the aid of CMEA countries represented 0.17
percent of GNP in 1982.[13]

Throughout this period, the United States was the single largest contributor of official development assistance. In 1982 it was responsible for 22 percent of ODA. That is almost double the contributions of each of the two second largest contributors: Japan and Saudi Arabia. But the goals and targets set by the development community are not measured by absolute contribution, but by the percentage of GNP given. By that measure, the United States ranked lowest of all DAC donors. Put another way, the U.S. had the second highest GNP per capita but one of the lowest percentages of GNP devoted to official development assistance of the seventeen DAC countries. Japan's percentage was only 0.33, whereas the contribution from Saudi Arabia was 3.53 percent of GNP. Only one country, Kuwait, had a better ratio at 4.46.[14]

Finally, note should be made of the proliferation of donors. When one adds together the bilateral, multilateral, and other funding sources, there are now more donors than there are recipient nations. Each donor has a slightly different type of project, and each has its own reporting requirements. Quite obviously, this places a considerable strain on the already stretched manpower of developing nations.

## CHANGING WESTERN PERCEPTIONS OF DEVELOPMENT ASSISTANCE

There is another important way in which circumstances have changed in the West since the initiation of aid programs in the early 'fifties: development assistance is not as popular as it was then. There are several reasons for this. Development has not happened as quickly or as smoothly as was anticipated following the success of the Marshall Plan. As one observer of the situation has pointed out:

> During the early euphoric years of capital transfers and technical missions, many experts believed that great improvements in levels of living could be obtained without completely restructuring the world's value systems, institutions and international relationships.[15]

To many at that time, development was synonymous with economic growth. In order to gain economic prosperity and technical modernity, less fortunate nations should emulate industrialized societies.

In the last several decades industrialized nations have begun to question the values, practices, structures,

and premises underlying the development process.
Environmental decay, natural catastrophes, ecological
crises, disputes over jurisdiction of the seas, population
explosion, the inescapable physical limits of natural
resources, to name just a few issues, have led to
widespread alienation in western nations in the quest for
more material wealth and greater economic expansion.  The
responsibility and obligation of the international
community to create conditions in which all nations have
greater access to resources is an increasingly popular
theme.

Perceptions in the developing world have also
changed.  People there are keenly aware of their poverty,
and some argue that their lack of development stems in
part from "structural" rigidities beyond their control.
As a consequence, they are due more aid from the
industrialized countries.  International political and
economic institutions and regulations favor industrialized
nations, they assert, making it difficult for Third World
nations to compete on equal terms.  A new international
economic order is needed to redistribute wealth, power,
and status among all nations of the world and rectify past
injustices.  Whatever the validity of this claim, it has
allowed developing countries to take on a new, more
positive identity and some reforms have occurred; however,
the claim has generated considerable irritation among
western leaders.

Second, as will be shown in the next chapter,
considerable development has taken place, with the result
that a number of developing countries are engaged in head-
to-head competition with western countries for markets.
And as long as the world is not operating at or near a
full employment level, these developing country
"successes" will be seen as competing with western
businesses and contributing to western unemployment.

Third, there is the perception in the West,
particularly in Europe, that development assistance is
contributing to a widening of income disparities in
developing countries.  These perceptions were fueled by a
series of International Labor Organization studies in the
late 'sixties and by rumors concerning the amounts various
developing country leaders have amassed in overseas
accounts.

On the political side, it was hoped that western aid
would generate more democratic institutions and less
instability and turmoil than has occurred.  The naivete of
this hope was pointed out ten years ago.  Nevertheless,

this is another instance in which reality did not live up to expectations.[16]

Finally, considerable distrust has grown up in all western nations, including the United States, regarding the motivations of the present U.S. government in using development assistance to buy political allegiance or to finance military activities either in support of or in opposition to governments in power.

Generally speaking, the citizens of western nations continue to express a desire to help less fortunate peoples of the world in their struggle to alleviate hunger and poverty. In 1983 the OECD reviewed public opinion polls taken in member countries since 1960. These polls indicate the general public continue to favor some form of foreign aid: "Even if people have somewhat mixed feelings about the developing countries, it is still considered right and proper to do something about hunger and poverty in the world."[17]

The recent drought in Africa, which resulted in starvation and drove millions of people deeper into poverty, generated intense public compassion and concern about the developed world. In 1983 two thousand mayors throughout France signed a petition calling for the allocation of greater resources to end world hunger. That same year the major voluntary organizations in Switzerland collected over 200,000 signatures on a petition to Parliament and the Federal Council not to cut the aid budget.[18] Further, there are the well-publicized efforts of rock musicians to raise money for relief in Ethiopia. Even in the United States, where public support for foreign aid has rarely risen above 50 percent, the vast majority of people support some form of humanitarian assistance to needy people around the globe. Nearly 60 percent of the respondents polled by the Chicago Council on Foreign Relations in 1982 said "combating world hunger" was a "very important" objective for the United States; only 5 percent felt it to be "not important."[19]

The success of the Marshall Plan in revitalizing the economies of Europe bred optimism that such accomplishments might be performed elsewhere. After forty years of economic assistance to the Third World, it is reasonable to ask whether the programs have achieved their objectives. Although there are clear indications that the standard of living in many nations has improved, it is equally obvious that there is a growing gap in perceptions of what might be accomplished and what should be accomplished. The traditional belief in the western world has been that the poor are disadvantaged because they are not part of the world political and economic system.  The task of the development expert was to reconstruct attitudes and institutions to reflect the West: then development would occur.  Westerners believed this would not be a zero-sum game: the West would also benefit from larger markets, the spread of democracy, and political stability.  Events have not confirmed this conviction.

There has been much change over the years: economic and political circumstances, the number of donors and their motives, the recipients of foreign aid and their needs.  The next two chapters will look at how economic conditions have changed in the Third World, how donor nations have altered allocations of official development assistance, and how development strategies have changed.

NOTES

1  A growing number of foreign aid observers are making this point.  See, for example, Stanley J. Heginbotham, "An Overview of U.S. Foreign Aid Programs," Congressional Research Service Report No. 85-87 F (Washington, D.C.: Library of Congress, 1985); Nick Eberstadt, "The Perversion of Foreign Aid," Commentary (June 1985), pp. 19-33.
2  Eberstadt, "The Perversion of Foreign Aid," p. 21.
3  For example, see E.M. Bernstein, "American Productivity and the Dollar Payments Problem," Review of Economics and Statistics (1955); R.N. Gardner, Sterling-Dollar Diplomacy (London: Oxford University Press, 1956).
4  John Naisbitt, Megatrends: Ten New Directions Transforming Our Lives (New York: Warner Books, Inc., 1982), p. 55.
5  For a review of the factors that influenced the architects of the early assistance efforts, see Massachusetts Institute of Technology, Center for International Studies, "The Objectives of United States Economic Assistance Programs," Study prepared for the Special Committee to Study the Foreign Aid Program, United States Senate, 85th Congress, 1st Session (January 1957), pp.4-15.
6  Ibid., pp. 11,12.
7  Francis Stewart, "The International Debt Situation and North-South Relations," World Development, Vol. 13, no. 2

(1985), p. 191.

[8] Naisbitt, Megatrends, p. 56; Lester C. Thurow, The Zero-Sum Society (New York: Penguin Books, 1981), p. 5.

[9] This issue will be discussed in chapter 5.

[10] Organization for Economic Co-operation and Development, Development Co-operation 1984 Review (Paris, 1984), p. 71.

[11] OECD, 1984 Review, pp. 81, 210.

[12] World Bank, World Development Report 1985 (Washington, D.C., 1985), p. 102.

[13] OECD, 1984 Review, p. 72.

[14] OECD, 1984 Review, pp. 207, 210, 212.

[15] Denis Goulet, The Cruel Choice: A New Concept in the Theory of Development (New York: Atheneum, 1977), p. 35.

[16] Samuel P. Huntington and Joan M. Nelson, No Easy Choice: Political Participation in Developing Countries (Cambridge: Harvard University Press, 1976).

[17] OECD, 1984 Review, p. 126.

[18] OECD, 1984 Review, p. 132.

[19] For evidence of the dichotomy between the way the American public views humanitarian relief in contrast to foreign aid in general, see Nick Eberstadt, "The Perversion of Foreign Aid," pp. 19-33.

# 2

# The Evolution of
# Developing Countries

Amazing changes have taken place in developing countries over the last three decades, and many of these changes have important implications for development assistance. A number of Asian and Latin American nations that were major recipients of foreign assistance in earlier days have emerged as world economic powers in their own right, and others are likely to follow shortly. A group of oil-producing countries have gone from being aid recipients to being significant donors. For other countries, growth has proceeded more slowly, if at all. This is particularly true on the African continent where the transition to independence was not always accompanied by adequate institutional development or prudent public policies.

The purpose of this chapter is to capture in aggregate fashion some of this change, or lack thereof, that has relevance for development assistance strategies, levels, and/or allocations. The aim is to provide an overview without getting caught up in country details. Hence, the review must be quantitative and focus on a small number of statistics. Of course, the prosperity of a country is multidimensional, and the various aspects of development are not easily captured in a small number of statistics.[1] However, by examining GNP, exports, and population it is possible to get some indication of a nation's competitive position internationally and the distribution of wealth domestically. Per capita GNP, with all its shortcomings, is still the single best aggregate measure of economic performance. The focus on exports is more debatable.[2] Although it is important to distinguish between those countries that followed an "outward-oriented" or export policy and those countries that spent

the last several decades developing a domestic import
substitution capacity, no attempt has been made to link
growth to a particular development strategy.

Overall, the growth record of developing countries
since the initiation of significant development assistance
efforts has been quite impressive.  Excluding the oil-
exporting countries and China, per capita incomes in real
terms grew by 2.8 percent annually during the 1960-1984
period.  It is interesting to compare this performance
with that of western nations during their industrial
transition.  The average annual growth of OECD nations
over the 1850-1960 period was only 1.8 percent in per
capita terms.  The growth rate of developing countries
over this earlier period was only 0.2 percent.  Of course,
these figures are totally inadequate when it comes to
establishing a causal link between aid and growth.  The
important point to note here is the rapid growth that has
taken place in developing countries over the last twenty-
five years.[3]

INCOME AND EXPORT GROWTH

A number of judgments had to be made concerning data
bases and categories of information here and in the
following chapters.  The data are presented by geographic
areas that conform closely to the regional categories
delineated by the OECD.  The one exception in this study
is the combination of African countries north of the
Sahara with Middle Eastern countries.  Not all countries
covered in the OECD reports are included in this data
base.  All European countries, North America, and
countries for which economic and population data are not
available are excluded.

Table 2.1
Income and Export Performance of Developing Regions, 1972-1982

| Region | GNP per Capita[a] 1982 $ | 1972-82 % Chge. | Exports 1982 $ mill. | 1982 % World | 1972-82 % Chge. |
|---|---|---|---|---|---|
| Africa, South of Sahara | 495 | -3 | 34029 | 2 | 317 |
| Middle East & Africa North of Sahara | 3062 | 47 | 152463 | 9 | 897 |
| Central America & the Caribbean | 1924 | 22 | 36617 | 2 | 532 |
| South America | 2108 | 24 | 60191 | 4 | 365 |
| Far East Asia | 505 | 56 | 155500 | 9 | 736 |
| South Asia | 249 | 21 | 13170 | 1 | 242 |
| TOTAL | 703 | 34 | 451970 | 27 | 599 |

Sources: OECD, 1984 Review and World Bank, World Development Report, 1985.
[a] GNP per capita figures are country averages weighted by population.

Table 2.1 presents per capita income and export
figures for various regional groupings of countries for
the years 1972 and 1982.[4] Several points stand out.
Overall, real per capita incomes grew by 34 percent or
roughly 3 percent annually, which is equivalent to growth
rates in industrial nations over the same period.
However, while world trade grew by more than 350 percent,
the international trade of these developing regions
increased almost twice as fast.  As a whole, developing
nations expanded exports from around 13 percent of GNP in
1970 to over 23 percent in 1983.  At the same time, the
composition of exports shifted from a predominance of
primary products to manufactured goods.[5] The sharp
increase in the Middle East derived almost exclusively
from higher oil prices.

The export performance of the Far East was truly
remarkable in that it was primarily the result of growth
in industries that compete directly with existing
industries in developed nations.  In both regions, per
capita income increased at a faster rate than in
industrialized nations.  Income and export growth were
also significant in South America.  In contrast, South
Asia, Central America, and the Caribbean registered very
modest income and trade gains, and the performance of
African nations south of the Sahara was quite
disappointing.  There was a 3 percent decline in per

14

capita income; the 2 percent share of world exports was
maintained only because of a sharp increase in Nigeria's
oil exports. Finally, it is worth noting that the two
regions with lowest per capita incomes, Africa and South
Asia, had the slowest growth in both income and exports.

While many developing countries have experienced
significant economic growth over the past several decades,
many have simultaneously incurred severe external debt
problems. Between 1970 and 1984 the debt of developing
countries increased to $686 billion, and the ability of
these countries as a whole to service their debts
deteriorated. The ratio of debt to GNP more than doubled;
interest payments on debt grew from 0.5 percent to 2.8
percent of GNP; the ratio of debt service to exports
increased from 14.7 percent to 19.7 percent.[6] As these
debts accumulate, developing nations have become more
vulnerable to external fluctuations in international
financial markets, and dependent upon the fiscal,
monetary, and trade policies of industrialized countries.
Although it is beyond the scope of this study to analyze
the international debt problem and consequent effects on
relations between developed and developing nations, it is
important to remember that a sizable reduction of growth
in a developing country will make debt-servicing even more
difficult and have profound implications for the borrower
and lender.[7]

Each of these regions will now be discussed in
detail.

## Far East Asia

The remarkable income and export performance of
Korea, Singapore, Taiwan, and Hong Kong during the 1972-
1982 decade demonstrates that being relatively resource-
poor does not exclude a nation from effectively competing
with the West in world industrial markets. Somewhat less
impressive but only by comparison was the performance of
China, Malaysia, and Thailand. Indonesia was able to
rapidly expand its exports, but much of this was the
result of increased oil sales. Only three countries in
the region had a larger percentage increase in exports
than tiny Macao.

It is interesting to reflect on the fact that until
quite recently, Korea, Taiwan, and Malaysia received
considerable amounts of development assistance. Thailand
is still a major recipient, and aid to China is now
increasing.

Table 2.2
Income and Export Performance of Far East Asian Countries

| | GNP per Capita | | Exports | | |
| Country | 1982 $ | 1972-82 % Chge. | 1982 $ mill. | 1982 % World | 1972-82 % Chge. |
|---------|------|---------|------|--------|---------|
| China | 310 | 55 | 21632 | 1.27 | 763 |
| Indonesia | 580 | 58 | 20004 | 1.18 | 1025 |
| Thailand | 800 | 49 | 7040 | 0.41 | 551 |
| Philippines | 820 | 36 | 5010 | 0.29 | 369 |
| Korea, Rep. | 1770 | 79 | 22251 | 1.31 | 1270 |
| Malaysia | 1840 | 60 | 11789 | 0.69 | 586 |
| Macao | 2500 | 239 | 743 | 0.04 | 946 |
| Taiwan | 2790 | 97 | 22204 | 1.30 | 662 |
| Hong Kong | 5340 | 97 | 20869 | 1.23 | 501 |
| Singapore | 5910 | 86 | 20787 | 1.22 | 850 |
| Brunei | 17880 | 106 | 3171 | 0.19 | 1702 |
| | | | | | |
| TOTAL | 505 | 56 | 155500 | 9.14 | 736 |

Sources: OECD, 1984 Review and World Bank, World
Development Report, 1985.

## South Asia

The slow growth of income and exports in the South
Asian countries stands in marked contrast to the Far East
region.  Overall, real per capita income grew more than
twice as rapidly in the Far East than in South Asia.  Out
of the entire southern group, only Sri Lanka had more
rapid growth in income than the Philippines, the slowest
growing country in the Far East. While the exports of the
Far East grew by more than 700 percent over the decade,
exports of the South Asian region increased by only 240
percent.  There were no fast-growing countries in this
area, but export growth in Nepal and Bangladesh was
slightly less than in the other nations.  As a whole,
South Asian countries have less than 1 percent of world
exports.

Table 2.3
Income and Export Performance of South Asian Countries

| | GNP per Capita | | Exports | | |
| | 1982 | 1972-82 | 1982 | 1982 | 1972-82 |
| Country | $ | % Chge. | $ mill. | % World | % Chge. |
|---|---|---|---|---|---|
| Bangladesh | 140 | 36 | 768 | 0.05 | 193 |
| Nepal | 170 | -5 | 46 | 0.00 | 92 |
| Burma | 190 | 34 | 390 | 0.02 | 217 |
| India | 250 | 17 | 8559 | 0.50 | 251 |
| Sri Lanka | 320 | 40 | 1033 | 0.06 | 220 |
| Pakistan | 380 | 33 | 2374 | 0.14 | 250 |
| | | | | | |
| TOTAL | 249 | 21 | 13170 | 0.77 | 242 |

Sources: OECD, 1984 Review and World Bank, World Development Report, 1985.


## Central America and the Caribbean

Aggregate income and export statistics for this region hide a wide variety of experiences. For example, while the exports of this region increased by 500 percent during the decade, most of this growth was the result of oil exports from Mexico. Excluding Mexico, exports increased by only 300 percent. It is interesting to note the rapid expansion of exports from Haiti, a country many development experts believe to be caught in a Malthusian poverty cycle. Haiti has appealed to foreign investors interested in setting up assembly activities because of its inexpensive labor, the ease of remitting profits (albeit illegally), and the nearness to the U.S. market.

Given the proximity of this region to the European and U.S. markets, more rapid growth could have been expected. However, relatively high wage rates, labor regulations, civil unrest, and readily available aid monies have hindered economic growth. On average, the increase in real per capita income was no better in this region than in South Asian countries. In four countries, El Salvador, Nicaragua, Jamaica, and the Bahamas, the decline in per capita income was significant.

Table 2.4
Income and Export Performance of Central American and Caribbean
Countries

| Country | GNP per Capita | | Exports | | |
| | 1982 $ | 1972-82 % Chge. | 1982 $ mill. | 1982 % World | 1972-82 % Chge. |
|---|---|---|---|---|---|
| Haiti | 300 | 12 | 380 | 0.02 | 805 |
| Honduras | 660 | 1 | 745 | 0.04 | 274 |
| El Salvador | 700 | -20 | 879 | 0.05 | 191 |
| Nicaragua | 900 | -29 | 366 | 0.02 | 47 |
| Belize | 1080 | 41 | 85 | 0.00 | 240 |
| Guatemala | 1140 | 12 | 1245 | 0.07 | 282 |
| Costa Rica | 1290 | -4 | 898 | 0.05 | 218 |
| Dominican Rep. | 1330 | 24 | 809 | 0.05 | 133 |
| Jamaica | 1350 | -28 | 858 | 0.05 | 129 |
| Panama | 1990 | 23 | 309 | 0.02 | 155 |
| Mexico | 2270 | 31 | 21163 | 1.24 | 1149 |
| Barbados | 2900 | 16 | 252 | 0.01 | 460 |
| Bahamas | 3830 | -13 | 1530 | 0.09 | 346 |
| Guadeloupe | 4200 | 49 | 99 | 0.01 | 148 |
| Martinique | 4680 | 31 | 137 | 0.01 | 191 |
| Neth. Antilles | 5150 | 14 | 3769 | 0.22 | 395 |
| Trin. & Tobago | 7140 | 60 | 3008 | 0.18 | 440 |
| Bermuda | 13200 | 22 | 85 | 0.00 | 136 |
| | | | | | |
| TOTAL | 1924 | 22 | 36617 | 2.15 | 532 |

Sources: OECD, 1984 Review and World Bank, World Development
Report, 1985.

## South America

Although real per capita incomes declined over the
decade in Bolivia, Guyana, Chile, Argentina, and Guiana,
other countries, particularly Ecuador, Colombia, Paraguay,
Brazil, and Suriname had an impressive record of income
growth. Regionally, exports grew by 365 percent over the
decade which represents an increased share of world trade.
Ecuador had the most impressive record, increasing exports
by 700 percent during this period, but again, most of this
came from oil sales. Venezuela, also helped by oil sales,
increased its exports by slightly more than 400 percent.
Brazil, by far the leading exporter of the region,
increased exports by 400 percent. Brazil's performance
was indeed impressive, even though it does not compare
with the performance of countries in the Far East region.

Table 2.5
Income and Export Performance of South American Countries

| Country | GNP per Capita | | Exports | | |
| | 1982 $ | 1972-82 % Chge. | 1982 $ mill. | 1982 % World | 1972-82 % Chge. |
|---|---|---|---|---|---|
| Bolivia | 570 | -7 | 732 | 0.04 | 205 |
| Guyana | 670 | -8 | 388 | 0.02 | 173 |
| Peru | 1200 | 1 | 3196 | 0.19 | 238 |
| Ecuador | 1350 | 48 | 2671 | 0.16 | 717 |
| Colombia | 1460 | 33 | 2992 | 0.18 | 245 |
| Paraguay | 1570 | 69 | 330 | 0.02 | 284 |
| Chile | 2210 | -16 | 3836 | 0.23 | 349 |
| Brazil | 2240 | 40 | 20168 | 1.18 | 404 |
| Argentina | 2530 | -10 | 7407 | 0.44 | 282 |
| Uruguay | 2650 | 15 | 1032 | 0.06 | 382 |
| Venezuela | 3080 | 1 | 17047 | 1.00 | 443 |
| Guiana | 3260 | -5 | 22 | 0.00 | 340 |
| Suriname | 3320 | 71 | 370 | 0.02 | 116 |
| TOTAL | 2108 | 24 | 60191 | 3.54 | 365 |

Sources: OECD, 1984 Review and World Bank, World Development Report, 1985.

## Middle East and North Africa

As mentioned earlier, exports of this region increased ninefold over the decade primarily as a result of the escalation of oil prices. Saudi Arabia's exports comprise about 50 percent of the region's total, and they increased by an even greater amount. It is notable that among the oil exporters Libya and Kuwait had relatively modest trade growth. The export growth rate for non-oil exporters was 330 percent, with Yemen PDR having the highest and Jordan having the lowest. As a group, these countries have about 9 percent of world exports, or the same volume as Far East Asian countries.

Because of the capital intensity and foreign ownership of the oil operations in many of these countries, exceptional export performance did not always mean impressive growth in per capita incomes. Libya and the United Arab Emirates illustrate this point. However, for the region overall, real incomes did rise an impressive 47 percent or roughly 4 percent annually.

Table 2.6
Income and Export Performance of Middle East and North
African Countries

| 1982 Country | GNP per Capita 1972-82 $ | 1982 % Chge. | Exports 1982 $ mill | 1972-82 % World | % Chge. |
|---|---|---|---|---|---|
| Yemen PDR | 470 | 95 | 580 | 0.03 | 1037 |
| Yemen Arab Rep. | 500 | 51 | 44 | 0.00 | 1000 |
| Egypt | 690 | 71 | 3120 | 0.18 | 278 |
| Morocco | 870 | 24 | 2130 | 0.13 | 233 |
| Tunisia | 1370 | 41 | 1974 | 0.12 | 535 |
| Jordan | 1680 | 122 | 563 | 0.03 | 1073 |
| Algeria | 2260 | 20 | 12533 | 0.74 | 874 |
| Israel | 5090 | -7 | 5287 | 0.31 | 360 |
| Oman | 5600 | 9 | 4115 | 0.24 | 1681 |
| Libya | 8510 | -20 | 12892 | 0.76 | 459 |
| Bahrain | 9280 | 128 | 3518 | 0.21 | 1642 |
| Saudi Arabia | 15520 | 69 | 77370 | 4.55 | 1612 |
| Kuwait | 19840 | 14 | 9797 | 0.58 | 236 |
| UAE | 23770 | -25 | 18540 | 1.09 | 2197 |
| TOTAL | 3062 | 47 | 152463 | 8.96 | 897 |

Sources: OECD, 1984 Review and World Bank, World Development
Report, 1985.

## Sub-Saharan Africa

In reviewing the performance of this region, the
dominant role of Nigeria should be kept in mind. That
country's GNP accounts for 44 percent of the region's
total. Including Nigeria, the total average regional per
capita income fell by 3 percent over the decade; without
Nigeria, real incomes fell by more than 5 percent.
Nigerian exports, which grew nearly 600 percent over the
decade because of oil sales, accounted for almost 45
percent of sub-Saharan exports in 1982. Excluding
Nigeria, sub-Saharan Africa's market share fell from 1.6
percent in 1972 to 1.1 percent ten years later. Except
for Nigeria, no country in this region had exports that
amounted to one-tenth of one percent of world exports.

20

Table 2.7
Income and Export Performance of African Countries South of
the Sahara

|  | GNP per Capita | | Exports | | |
|  | 1982 | 1972-82 | 1982 | 1982 | 1972-82 |
| Country | $ | % Chge. | $ mill | % World | % Chge. |
| Chad | 80 | -56 | 101 | 0.01 | 181 |
| Ethiopia | 140 | 5 | 400 | 0.02 | 140 |
| Gu.-Bissau | 170 | -14 | 10 | 0.00 | 233 |
| Mali | 180 | 7 | 93 | 0.01 | 121 |
| Zaire | 190 | -25 | 1713 | 0.10 | 132 |
| Malawi | 210 | 12 | 232 | 0.01 | 186 |
| Upper Volta | 210 | 15 | 80 | 0.00 | 300 |
| Uganda | 230 | -31 | 371 | 0.02 | 31 |
| Rwanda | 260 | 26 | 82 | 0.00 | 332 |
| Burundi | 280 | 24 | 88 | 0.01 | 238 |
| Tanzania | 280 | 0 | 480 | 0.03 | 50 |
| Somalia | 290 | -1 | 143 | 0.01 | 233 |
| Benin | 310 | 13 | 34 | 0.00 | -6 |
| Central Afr. Rep. | 310 | -9 | 106 | 0.01 | 165 |
| Guinea | 310 | 5 | 411 | 0.02 | 793 |
| Niger | 310 | -1 | 307 | 0.02 | 469 |
| Madagascar | 320 | -25 | 433 | 0.03 | 164 |
| Togo | 340 | -2 | 213 | 0.01 | 326 |
| Cape Verde | 350 | 3 | 3 | 0.00 | 50 |
| Ghana | 360 | -34 | 929 | 0.05 | 116 |
| Kenya | 390 | 6 | 1125 | 0.07 | 212 |
| Sierra Leone | 390 | -2 | 169 | 0.01 | 42 |
| Sudan | 440 | -21 | 583 | 0.03 | 63 |
| Mauritania | 470 | 0 | 256 | 0.02 | 139 |
| Liberia | 490 | -16 | 1200 | 0.07 | 344 |
| Senegal | 490 | -3 | 482 | 0.03 | 122 |
| Zambia | 640 | -24 | 880 | 0.05 | 16 |
| Nigeria | 860 | 2 | 14901 | 0.88 | 584 |
| Cameroon | 890 | 47 | 1721 | 0.10 | 648 |
| Zimbabwe | 940 | 1 | 1057 | 0.06 | 1115 |
| Ivory Coast | 950 | 4 | 2441 | 0.14 | 347 |
| Congo | 1180 | 40 | 923 | 0.05 | 1147 |
| Seychelles | 1960 | 28 | 34 | 0.00 | 1600 |
| Gabon | 4000 | -1 | 1946 | 0.11 | 908 |
| Reunion | 4010 | -1 | 82 | 0.00 | 61 |
| TOTAL | 495 | -1 | 34029 | 2.00 | 317 |

Sources: OECD, 1984 Review and World Bank, World Development
Report, 1985.

SUMMARY

In retrospect, the economic progress of developing countries has been quite remarkable since the initiation of significant development assistance efforts. For the decade examined above, real per capita incomes in developing countries grew at the same overall rate as incomes in the developed world. By the end of the decade, forty-six of the countries examined above had per capita incomes in excess of $1000. However, there were a rather large number of lower-income developing countries that appear to have been left behind. Yet some policy makers argue that there is no longer a sensible justification for providing development assistance to the emerging nations, particularly when it appears western jobs are being directly threatened by some of these countries. Before reaching this conclusion, it is worth looking at other data. The next chapter will trace how per capita income changes have been related to variations in official development assistance allocations over the last decade, and briefly review shifts in donor approaches and strategies.

NOTES

[1] For a recent statistical examination of the relationship between economic and noneconomic variables, see Rati Ram, "The Role of Real Income Level and Income Distribution in Fulfillment of Basic Needs," World Development, Vol. 13, no. 5 (1985), pp. 589-593. Concerning the relationship between economic variables and subjective measures of quality of life, see Hadley Cantril, The Patterns of Concerns (New Brunswick: Rutgers University Press, 1965).
[2] For a discussion of the positive and negative attributions of export oriented growth in the past, present, and future, see Gustav Ranis, "Can the East Asian Model of Development be Generalized?" World Development, Vol. 13, no. 4 (1985), pp. 543-546; William R. Cline, "Reply," ibid., pp. 547-548. Also see, Bela Belassa, "Adjustment Policies in Developing Countries: A Reassessment," World Development, Vol. 12, no. 9 (1984), pp. 955-972.
[3] These figures come from OECD, 1985 Review. For another examination of developing countries' growth, see David

Morawetz, Twenty-five Years of Economic Development: 1950
to 1975 (Washington, D.C.: World Bank, 1977).
[4] Reasonably, it can be argued that a longer time should
have been studied. This period is long enough, however, to
highlight the important changes that took place. Also,
there are serious data problems if a longer period is
chosen.
[5] World Bank, World Development Report, 1985, pp. 21, 23.
[6] Ibid., p. 2.
[7] For an analysis of the debt issue, see Francis Stewart,
"The International Debt Situation and North-South
Relations," pp. 191-204.

# 3

## Changing Development Strategies and Aid Allocations

Numerous reports have charted the course of changing development strategies.[1] Unfortunately, there has not been a corresponding flow of studies to assess the impact of these strategies. This might appear odd, given the large number of evaluation activities, both past and present.

There appear to be a number of reasons for the lack of useful evaluation material. First, the vast preponderance of evaluation monies have been spent on the assessment of individual projects and/or programs. Second, the evaluation methodologies that have been employed are rarely powerful enough to isolate the effects of development assistance from other forces contributing to development. Third, the evaluations have generally been done at or before project or program completion, and this is usually too soon to make even an educated guess regarding impact. Fourth, it is not possible to make the sorts of comparative assessments required to derive general conclusions about development impact from an ex post review of completed evaluations. And finally, much of the published work of donors assessing their own performance has been defensive, self-serving, and promotional.[2] Nevertheless, the question of impact is important and in what follows, an attempt is made to say something useful, albeit subjective, on this matter.

REVIEWING THE RECORD

For purposes of review, it is useful to divide development assistance into three distinct periods: 1950 to 1972, 1973 to 1980, and 1981 to the present. Before considering each of these eras it is important to distinguish between the rhetoric and what changes actually occurred in field operations. For example, the strategies introduced in the 'seventies called for basic changes in development approaches, and the vehicle for these changes were projects. However, probably less than 10 percent of the project portfolio of any major donor has ever reflected the characteristics called for by this new approach to development.[3] In part, this is a reflection of bureaucratic inertia within donor organizations that is compounded by the distances between headquarters and field operations; in part, it is a reflection of prior commitments in the existing portfolio; and in part it reflects a lack of understanding of how to translate the rhetoric of a new approach into an operational program. In fact, some critics of donor organizations have argued development programs are reclassified to comply with legislative mandates, but change very little.[4] According to one report, for example, the World Bank's claim that it greatly increased the amount of money directed at helping the poor in agriculture and nutrition programs in response to the 1973 new approach was misleading. Funds were allocated to the agricultural sector, but much of the money was used as it had been previously: for roads, infrastructure development, and equipment.[5]

This does not mean that over a period of years there have not been important shifts in development strategies. There is no question that the approaches taken in the years immediately following the Marshall Plan were significantly different than what was promoted in the 'seventies, and that now new priorities are being reflected in donor activities.[6] But programmatic changes occur slowly and are extremely difficult to measure. aThe wide variety of approaches and programs among the donors and use of terms and definitions complicates the analysis. The point is a historical review of changes in development thinking and announced strategies gives an exaggerated impression of the actual shifts in donor activities. To give a general setting for the discussion on foreign assistance allocations, let us briefly summarize development trends.

## 1950 - 1972

In many ways the initial period of development
assistance to the Third World reflected the strategies of
the Marshall Plan.  Most economic assistance during this
time emphasized resource transfers that were used to
provide essential physical infrastructure.  But in
contrast to the Marshall Plan, technical assistance was
provided.  Attention was focused on the importance of
sound economic planning and other forms of technical work.
Effort also went into building human resources through
higher education and research capabilities.

As mentioned previously, the United States initially
provided virtually all development assistance, both
bilateral and multilateral.  By the 'seventies, other
donors had become important players in both bilateral and
multilateral assistance activities.  Near the end of this
period serious questions were raised about the impact and
appropriateness of this derivative form of development aid
based on the strategies articulated in the Marshall Plan.
However, considerable time passed before any significant
changes were made in the development assistance portfolio
to reflect these criticisms.

## 1973 - 1980

A number of studies were written in the late 'sixties
suggesting that income differentials were widening in
developing countries and that the "poorest of the poor"
were being left behind.[7]  These studies in part served as
the basis for a change in programmatic emphasis that was
reflected in virtually all development assistance
agencies.  The new objective was to target economic
assistance directly to the poorest segments of developing
countries living in rural areas; the standard vehicle was
a project intended to improve the income of the rural
poor.  Old slogans supporting macroeconomic planning and
"trickle-down development" were out; participatory,
bottom-up development employing appropriate technologies
that provided for "basic human needs" was the new theory
in vogue.  These phrases covered a wide array of
approaches devised by various donors to provide
development assistance directly to the rural poor.

Equally important were the institutional changes in
the manner that aid was packaged and delivered.  The
number of donors proliferated, and they became
increasingly insistent on specifying exactly how their

assistance could be used.  Often, donors activities became
narrowly defined as legislators enacted amendments to the
laws governing foreign aid.  In earlier times, a
developing country might have two or three donors to deal
with, each of whom provided a significant amount of
program money to be spent in accordance with general
guidelines.  By the end of this period, a country the size
of Lesotho had to deal with more than fifty donors and a
project portfolio that exceeded three hundred.  As we once
said, the most important difference between development
assistance in the 1970s and earlier decades was not the
emphasis on the rural poor and the participatory
approaches but the effects of institutional destruction
resulting from donor and project proliferation.[8]

## 1981 - present

By the end of the 'seventies, there was little
evidence that the targeted, bottom-up approach to
development was having a significant impact.  It seemed
apparent that there was need to focus again on
macroeconomic policies and to improve the capacity of
institutions in Third World countries.  Criticism of the
"new" approaches concentrated primarily on their failure
to promote economic policies that would allow free markets
and private sector activities to flourish.[9]  Little
attention went to evaluating the potential of these
strategies for providing long-term economic development.[10]
Changes in domestic politics in the United States in
1980 introduced a new ideological purpose for the foreign
assistance program of that country that were not apparent
in other major western donors.  Whereas in the past, it
had been argued that U.S. foreign policy interests would
be best served by a program that provided aid for economic
development,[11] there was evidence as the 1980s progressed
that U.S. foreign policy objectives would best be achieved
by providing "security assistance" to political allies.[12]
A presidential commission recommended closer integration
of the U.S. security program i.e., military assistance,
and economic development assistance.[13]  Aside from the
hoped for political allegiances that might result from
such a focus, from a purely development perspective,
military aid detracts from funds available for development
assistance.  There are several reasons why this happens.
As can be seen in table 3.1, the debt service on loans for
arms purchases can become quite large.  In the case of
Turkey, for example, the debt service on military

purchases amounted to 197 percent of the economic aid received in 1985; in Israel it was almost 90 percent of the economic assistance package. Military and economic assistance debts must be paid in hard currencies. So must many of the recurrent costs of maintaining military equipment and development assistance programs. As the recipients of military and economic aid have limited international reserves, the escalation of the debt service creates a situation in which national military and economic development requirements will compete for scarce hard currencies.

Table 3.1
Economic Assistance and Debt Service on Military Purchases
For Selected Countries, 1985
($ millions)

| Country | New Military Loans and Grants | Debt Service on Arms Purchases | Economic Assistance | Debt Service as a % of Economic Aid |
|---|---|---|---|---|
| Israel | 1400.0 | 1068.0 | 1200.0 | 89.0 |
| Egypt | 1177.0 | 659.8 | 1052.0 | 62.7 |
| Turkey | 703.1 | 345.5 | 175.0 | 197.4 |
| Pakistan | 325.9 | 66.1 | 300.0 | 22.0 |
| Thailand | 102.3 | 46.3 | 28.5 | 162.5 |
| El Salvador | 128.3 | 21.2 | 317.1 | 6.7 |

Sources: U.S. State Department and U.S. Center for Defense Information.

Other western donor nations also provide military assistance, but their foreign aid programs are still primarily directed at improving economic conditions. In part this is a result of recent droughts and famine, but also it is the result of need and national political philosophy. However, with high levels of unemployment in most western nations, many donors are placing more emphasis on obtaining trade payoffs from the provision of foreign assistance.

ASSESSING THE RECORD

From a review of the incomplete documentation of development assistance since its inception in the 'fifties, several observations are possible. A large number of countries, particularly in Asia and Latin

America, have made significant development progress. This
progress is reflected in social and economic indicators as
well as the ability to compete internationally in
industrial markets. It is not, however, possible to
causally link this progress directly to foreign aid and
the strategies associated therewith. Many of these
emerging nations received large public resource transfers
from the United States during the first development
assistance era; they also received considerable formal and
informal advice from Americans on development policies and
strategies. In later years, these countries have been the
recipients of considerable foreign capital from private
sources. These experiences might lead one to infer that
the early public inflows provided the necessary physical
and intellectual infrastructure to make these countries
attractive to private foreign capital at a later date.

It is more difficult to infer that the development
strategies adopted in the 'seventies had positive
consequences of a similar magnitude. A major tenet of the
supporters of participatory, targeted development
assistance to the poor was that the benefits of more
traditional approaches did not "trickle down" to the
needy. While there are certain countries where this
assertion clearly applies, one of the few comprehensive
reviews of development efforts suggests the opposite: that
the benefits of nontargeted development tend to reach
nearly all segments of society.[14] Of course, in theory,
conditions could be much better: even in western nations,
pockets of severe poverty remain.

A more serious indictment of the supporters of the
basic needs strategies is their dismissal of other
approaches before there was any evidence to indicate that
the concepts they were promoting could be made operational
by donor agencies so that large numbers of persons living
in poverty in the developing world would benefit. To this
day, there is virtually no evidence to suggest donors can
make these concepts work.

Finally, supporters of these new approaches were
generally quite dogmatic about what should be done.
Having seen the obvious defects of past western
development efforts and having acquired new perceptions of
international responsibilities and expectations, they
wanted to try something different. The developing world
provided them with such an opportunity. But donors failed
to consider that providing for basic needs is not likely
to become a self-financing set of activities. Further,
the effect of providing for these needs might have serious

consequences for population growth and work incentives.[15]
But it is easy to be overly critical.  The emphasis on
basic human needs stems from the recognition that there
are millions of people living in conditions of deprivation
and suffering, and the desire to do something about it.
To the extent that low-cost, sustainable service delivery
systems can be developed that alleviate some of this
misery, a tremendous number of people will benefit.

The 'seventies were also a period in which donors
gave far too little attention to the importance of
economic policies employed by developing countries.  They
sponsored a wide range of rural projects that were
intended to generate income.  It was only after this had
been going on for some time that donors recognized that
government policies in many developing countries were
exploiting rural people for the benefit of urban elites
with the result that there was insufficient income flowing
to rural areas to create income generating activities.
Recognition that these anti-rural policies did not lead to
income generating activities did not produce an immediate
change in donor policies.  For example, when donors found
that there were no technological packages that would be
attractive to farmers at prevailing producer prices, they
moved to subsidize other productive inputs rather than
applying pressure to governments to increase prices.  This
led to a situation at the end of the 'seventies in which a
large portion of donor-sponsored agricultural/rural
development activities had no prospect of becoming self-
sustaining and could only be maintained through a
continuation of massive donor subsidies.

There are other reasons for finding fault with
development activities in the 'seventies and 'eighties.
It was a period in which many donors began to specify
precisely how their money was to be used; it was also a
time in which the types of things donors wanted done
expanded, as did the number of donors. This growth in
donors, donor initiatives and requirements had the effect
of fragmenting governmental institutions, programs, and
policies of many developing countries.  Not being in a
position to resist the wide and often inconsistent array
of donor demands and activities, governments capitulated
and thereby lost the opportunity to evolve their own sets
of policies and programs.  This fact has now been
recognized, and efforts are underway to increase the
coordination of donor activities.  However, the jury is
still out on whether significant steps to increase
coordination will be taken and maintained.  Ultimately,

problems will not be resolved by better donor
coordination.  The real test will be whether donors are
willing to alter fundamental attitudinal and behavioral
patterns and promote and support efforts by developing
country governments to evolve their own development
strategies.  Such changes will not be easy to
institutionalize.[16]

ALLOCATIONS OF DEVELOPMENT ASSISTANCE

Having briefly reviewed the changes in development
strategies, past and present allocations of official
development assistance will now be examined.

In table 3.2 one sees an overall picture of how
official development assistance, gross national product
(GNP), and population are distributed among the regional
groupings.  As can be seen, the percentage of aid going to
Africa and the Middle East significantly increased in the
ten year period.  Taken together, their share expanded
from 29 percent in 1972 to 53 percent of the aggregate aid
in 1982.  During the same period, the population in these
two regions decreased from 15 to 11 percent of the world's
total.  India is included in the South Asian region, which
explains the large population in this area, and China is
included in Far East Asia.  Together these regions have 88
percent of the world's population and receive 31 percent
of official development assistance.

Table 3.2
Percent Distribution of ODA, GNP, and Population for 1972
and 1982

| | ODA | | GNP | | Population | |
|---|---|---|---|---|---|---|
| Region | 1972 | 1982 | 1972 | 1982 | 1972 | 1982 |
| Africa South of Sahara | 18 | 32 | 10 | 8 | 11 | 9 |
| Middle East and Africa North of Sahara | 11 | 21 | 14 | 18 | 4 | 2 |
| South Asia | 13 | 21 | 12 | 11 | 30 | 38 |
| Far East Asia | 22 | 10 | 25 | 29 | 45 | 50 |
| Oceania | 4 | 4 | 1 | a | a | a |
| Central America and The Caribbean | 10 | 8 | 10 | 10 | a | 1 |
| South America | 22 | 5 | 27 | 24 | 8 | a |
| TOTALS[b] | 11943 | 22957 | 1190260 | 2084205 | 2541 | 3152 |

Sources: ODA data come from various OECD Reviews. GNP and
population data come from issues of the World Bank, World
Development Report.
[a] Less than half of 1 percent.
[b] ODA and GNP totals are $ millions. Population
totals are in millions.

The data in table 3.3 invite some interesting
comparisons. Overall, the importance of aid relative to
the recipient countries own economic activity (GNP)
increased slightly from 1.0 to 1.1 percent. However, ODA
remains a very small portion of resources, suggesting that
aid can only really serve as a catalyst to domestic
development efforts. Among country groupings Africa, the
Middle East, South Asia, and Oceania increased the portion
of aid to GNP over the decade. It decreased in the Far
East, Central America, the Caribbean, and South America
largely as a result of economic progress in these regions.
    In real terms, per capita aid for all regions fell
from $9 to $7 over the decade. Only Africa, the Middle
East, and South Asia received increases in per capita
assistance. Significantly less per capita aid went to
Asia and South America than to other developing regions.

Table 3.3
Development Assistance Ratios for All Countries, 1972
and 1982

| Region | ODA/GNP For All Countries[a] | | Real[b] ODA/P For All Countries | |
|--------|------|------|------|------|
|  | 1972 | 1982 | 1972 | 1982 |
| Africa South of Sahara | 1.80 | 4.54 | 16 | 20 |
| Middle East and Africa North of Sahara | 0.77 | 1.27 | 28 | 38 |
| South Asia | 1.02 | 2.09 | 4 | 5 |
| Far East Asia | 0.09 | 0.04 | 5 | 2 |
| Oceania | 7.38 | 10.50 | 295 | 194 |
| Central America and Caribbean | 1.01 | 0.91 | 29 | 17 |
| South America | 0.81 | 0.21 | 27 | 4 |
| TOTAL | 1.00 | 1.10 | 9 | 7 |

Source: OECD, 1984 Review.
[a] In percentages.
[b] The OECD GNP deflator was used in this table and the
remainder of the report to convert 1972 aid outlays to
1982 dollars. In this study, the term "real" means ODA
data have been adjusted accordingly.

One would expect some variation in the allocation of
aid dependent upon different inter-regional levels of
development. For example, it can be hypothesized that
less aid would go to a region that had countries with high
per capita incomes, and more aid would go to a region
where most countries had low per capita income levels.
With this in mind, aid recipients were examined on the
basis of whether their per capita incomes were above or
below $850, a figure close to the ceiling on International
Development Association (IDA) loans; also, it is
considered a reasonable dividing point between emerging
and less well-off developing nations.[17]
The next two tables present aid for nations with per
capita incomes less than $850 standardized for GNP and
population, respectively. In addition, these tables show
the ratio or differential of official development

assistance for countries with a GNP less than $850 per
capita to countries with a GNP of more than $850 per
capita. A differential of one indicates that countries
below and above the $850 GNP per capita cut-off are
receiving equivalent amounts of aid.

Looking at table 3.4, it appears that when developing
countries are taken together, the ODA/GNP differential
doubled from 1972 to 1982. That is, while rich and poorer
countries received about the same amount of aid
standardized by GNP in 1972 (a differential of 0.98), the
poorer countries received almost twice as much by 1982 (a
differential of 1.90). For African countries south of the
Sahara, the situation moved from equality to a
differential of 2.14. The differential also jumped
substantially for countries in the Middle East, North
Africa, Central America, and the Caribbean. In the South
Asian case there is no differential inasmuch as all
countries are poor nations. The poorer developing nations
in Far East Asia and South America received less aid
relative to their GNPs than the other regional groups.

In sum, the ODA/GNP ratio for richer and poorer
nations was about the same in 1972. By 1982 the ratio for
poorer countries had become twice that of the richer
nations.

Table 3.4
ODA/GNP Percentages for Nations with a GNP Less than $850/Capita,
1972, 1982

| Region | 1972 ODA/GNP[a] (%) | 1972 ODA/GNP[b] Differential | 1982 ODA/GNP[a] (%) | 1982 ODA/GNP[b] Differential |
|---|---|---|---|---|
| Africa South of Sahara | 1.9 | 1.05 | 9.7 | 2.14 |
| Middle East and Africa North of Sahara | 0.8 | 0.99 | 5.8 | 4.59 |
| South Asia | 1.0 | c | 2.1 | c |
| Far East Asia | 0.6 | 0.64 | 0.5 | 1.33 |
| Oceania | 14.1 | 1.91 | 13.9 | 1.32 |
| Central America and Caribbean | 0.2 | 0.21 | 6.4 | 7.05 |
| South America | 1.2 | 1.45 | 2.7 | 12.59 |
| TOTAL | 1.0 | 0.98 | 2.1 | 1.90 |

Source: OECD, 1984 Review.
[a] Nations with a GNP per capita less than $850.
[b] Ratio of ODA/GNP of countries with a GNP less than $850 per
capita to countries with a GNP more than $850 per capita.
[c] Not available.

Table 3.5 shows the dollar amount of aid per person
in the poorer (GNP/P less than $850) developing countries.
In real terms, per capita aid levels have risen from $4 to
$6 for the poorer nations.  The per capita level in
Oceania, which includes a number of "countries" still
under the direction of a developed nation from which they
receive substantial sums, is extremely high.  In contrast,
Far East Asian countries received very small amounts of
aid.  The per capita amounts received by the poorer South
American countries are closer to the African levels than
to those of Asia.

The table also provides the ODA/P differentials
between rich and poorer developing nations.  In comparison
with the previous table, the differentials are smaller.
Putting it slightly differently, it is notable that for
both periods, richer developing nations received more aid
per capita than poorer ones.  However, the differential
did fall from 48 to 86 percent.  In 1982 the differential
favored poorer nations in Africa south of the Sahara,
Central America and the Caribbean, and South America.

Table 3.5
Real ODA/P for Nations with a GNP Less than $850/Capita,
1972, 1982

| | 1972[a] | | 1982 | |
| Region | ODA/P | Differential | ODA/P | Differential |
|---|---|---|---|---|
| Africa South of Sahara | 14 | 0.89[b] | 25 | 1.24[b] |
| Middle East and Africa North of Sahara | 8 | 0.31 | 37 | 0.97 |
| South Asia | 4 | NA | 5 | NA |
| Far East Asia | 2 | 0.50 | 2 | 0.98 |
| Oceania | 145 | 0.49 | 100 | 0.52 |
| Central America and Caribbean | 4 | 0.13 | 35 | 2.13 |
| South America | 26 | 0.99 | 28 | 6.55 |
| TOTAL | 4 | 0.48 | 6 | 0.86 |

Source: OECD, 1984 Review.
[a] In 1982 U.S. dollars.
[b] Ratio of ODA/P of countries with a GNP less than $850 per
capita to countries with a GNP more than $850 per capita.

To get a better sense of changes in allocations of
aid, it is often instructive to examine the extreme cases,
that is, countries receiving the largest and smallest
amounts of ODA relative to GNP and population. This is
done in the following two tables, which also include a GNP
per capita figure to give a perspective on relative levels
of poverty.

Table 3.6 presents the countries which rank in the
top ten on either the ODA/GNP ratio or per capita aid.[18]
As one might expect, African countries dominate the
picture. In Cape Verde and Somalia, official aid is equal
to an astonishing 50 percent of the national income.
However, the list also includes several Middle East oil
countries whose presence is clearly a function of
political or security concerns and not poverty
considerations. Take, for example, Bahrain with a GNP per
capita of $9300. It received $219 per person in 1982
whereas Mali, with an annual per capita income of $180,
got only $28 per person in aid.

Table 3.6
Countries with the Highest ODA/GNP and ODA/P
Ratios, 1982

| Country | ODA/GNP | ODA/P | GNP/P |
|---|---|---|---|
| Cape Verde | 49.91 | 183[a] | 350[a] |
| Somalia | 49.69 | 102 | 290 |
| Guinea-Bissau | 48.71 | 80 | 170 |
| Comoros | 35.91 | 107 | 340 |
| Mauritania | 26.31 | 112 | 470 |
| Mali | 18.95 | 28 | 180 |
| Solomon Islands | 17.75 | 114 | 650 |
| Niger | 16.79 | 43 | 310 |
| Lesotho | 14.93 | 64 | 530 |
| Seychelles | 14.23 | 308 | 1960 |
| Jordan | 13.85 | 232 | 1680 |
| Suriname | 8.25 | 290 | 3320 |
| Israel | 4.34 | 213 | 5090 |
| Bahrain | 2.36 | 219 | 9280 |
| Oman | 2.31 | 128 | 5600 |

Source: OECD, 1984 Review.
[a] In 1982 U.S. dollars.

     Table 3.7 shows countries with the lowest levels of
either ODA/GNP or per capita aid.  Again per capita income
is included.  This table is composed of a number of large
Asian countries with vast populations; in addition, it
includes Bolivia and a handful of African countries that
have been going through a series of political upheavals.
It also includes two Asian countries, Bhutan and Burma,
that have until recently been closed to the West.
     From a comparison of tables 3.6 and 3.7, it would
appear that size and population are important determinants
for the amount of aid received.  The average size of the
countries with the highest ratios of aid to population and
gross national product is 128,445 square miles; the
average size of the countries with the smallest ratio is
598,271 square miles.
     The average per capita income of the countries
receiving the least amounts of aid is much lower than the
average for the countries receiving the most aid; the
average per capita income for the countries appearing in
table 3.6 is $2015; for countries appearing in table 3.7,
the average is $370.

Table 3.7
Countries with the Lowest ODA/GNP and ODA/P Ratios,
1982

-----------------------------------------------------
| Country | ODA/GNP | ODA/P | GNP/P |
|---|---|---|---|
| China | 0.20 | 1[a] | 310[a] |
| Philippines | 0.85 | 7 | 820 |
| India | 0.91 | 2 | 250 |
| Indonesia | 1.04 | 6 | 580 |
| Thailand | 1.09 | 8 | 800 |
| Bolivia | 2.27 | 25 | 570 |
| Pakistan | 2.76 | 10 | 380 |
| Ghana | 3.31 | 12 | 350 |
| Guinea | 4.07 | 13 | 340 |
| Ethiopia | 4.51 | 6 | 140 |
| Bhutan | 7.53 | 8 | 120 |
| Burma | 5.45 | 9 | 190 |
| Uganda | 4.85 | 10 | 240 |

Source: OECD, 1984 Review.
[a] In 1982 US dollars.

Another measure of aid allocations is presented in
table 3.8.  It provides by region a comparison of the
percentage of aid going to countries with real per capita
incomes less or more than $850 in 1972 and 1982.  Overall
in 1982, 69 percent of ODA went to poorer countries versus
43 percent in 1972, an increase of 26 percent.  With the
exception of the sub-Saharan African group, the percentage
was higher in all groups in the latter year.  In sub-
Saharan Africa it was lower largely because of the
continuation or increase in aid to four countries that
moved above the $850 ceiling between 1972 and 1982: the
Congo, Botswana, Cameroon, and Nigeria.  The improvement
in the Middle East/North Africa region was largely the
result of U.S. aid to Egypt which increased its net ODA
inflow from $14 million in 1972 to $1.4 billion in 1982.
The South Asian region does not include any country with
per capita income greater than $850.
    The increase in the poor countries' share in the Far
East region is due to the virtual elimination of aid to
four countries that had per capita incomes in excess of
$850 in both periods: Hong Kong, Singapore, South Korea,
and Taiwan.  In 1972 these countries received $1.2 billion
in ODA; in 1982 they netted only $56 million.

Table 3.8
The Percent Distribution of ODA Among Richer/Poorer
Developing Nations, 1972 and 1982

| Region | % ODA to Poorer Nations 1972 | 1982 | % ODA to Richer Nations 1972 | 1982 |
|---|---|---|---|---|
| Africa South of Sahara | 96 | 82 | 4 | 18 |
| Middle East and Africa North of Sahara | 16 | 42 | 84 | 58 |
| South Asia | 100 | 100 | 0 | 0 |
| Far East Asia | 47 | 92 | 53 | 8 |
| Oceania | 3 | 39 | 97 | 61 |
| Central America and Caribbean | 1 | 27 | 99 | 73 |
| South America | 3 | 5 | 97 | 95 |
| TOTAL | 43 | 69 | 57 | 31 |

Source: OECD, 1984 Review.

The Solomon Islands was the only country in the
Oceania group with average per capita income less than
$850 in both periods.  Its ODA more than doubled between
1972 and 1982.  However, the most important reason for the
increase in the poor country share of this region was the
movement of Papua New Guinea from the rich to the poor
category in 1982.  This moved more than $300 million of
ODA into the poor category.
     The only countries with per capita incomes less than
$850 in Central America and the Caribbean in both years
were Haiti and Honduras.  These countries were joined in
the poor income category in 1982 by El Salvador.  In
aggregate, these countries netted only $33 million of ODA
in 1972; by 1982, their ODA increased to $504 million.
Mexico, a country with average per capita income in excess
of $850 in both years, received $368 million in 1972; in
1982, it was still receiving $140 million of ODA.
     In the South American region, only two countries,
Guyana and Bolivia, had per capita incomes less than $850
in either 1972 or 1982, and in both countries per capita
incomes fell over the decade.  By 1982, aside from these

two countries, the lowest per capita income in the region
was $1200 for Peru.  Eleven countries with per capita
incomes between $1200 and $3320 received $863 million in
official aid.

PRELIMINARY FINDINGS ON ALLOCATIONS OF AID

In 1982, 30 percent or $7 billion of official
development assistance went to countries with per capita
incomes in excess of $850.  Countries with incomes above
the $850 level are getting more aid per capita than poorer
nations.  A greater share of multilateral concessionary
aid goes to the poorer countries than is the case for
bilateral aid.  However, most of the nonconcessionary
multilateral assistance goes to wealthier nations.
Developing countries in both Far East and South Asia
get far less aid relative to population or income than
developing nations in other regions of the world.  This is
true of countries both above and below the $850 per capita
income level.
Aid levels are relatively high in Africa, the Middle
East, Central America, and the Caribbean.  Indeed, one
might wonder whether these levels exceed absorptive
capacities, given existing aid forms and delivery
mechanisms, and whether in turn they could be in the
process of creating serious dependency relationships.

CONCLUSIONS

After reviewing the allocations of official
development assistance and changes in development
strategies over the last several decades, it would appear
that development assistance is not guided by a thoroughly
rational system or analysis.  While political, historical,
humanitarian, strategic, economic, and military
considerations will always play important roles in a
donor's decisions regarding aid allocations, it is worth
asking whether, from a global perspective, there is any
truly rational basis for making allocations of aid among
countries that would be acceptable to the majority of
donors.  For example, can a reasonable argument be made
for providing relatively more aid to smaller and or richer
countries, as is now the case, than vice versa?  So also,
it is reasonable to ask whether better guidance can be
offered on how aid monies should be spent.
The next section of this book looks into the future
and explores some of the issues involved in answering
these questions.

NOTES

[1] For example, see Elliott R. and Victoria A. Morss, U.S. Foreign Aid: An Assessment of New and Traditional Development Strategies (Boulder: Westview Press, 1982).

[2] For interesting comments on the paucity of good evaluation in the field of foreign assistance see, Guy Gran, Development by People: Citizen Construction of a Just World (New York: Praeger Publishers, 1983), pp. 291-325.

[3] See Elliott Morss, "Bilateral Development Cooperation and the Programmatic Approach," Report prepared for the Institute of Social Studies Advisory Staff (The Hague, 1982).

[4] Increased use of computers greatly facilitates such reclassification efforts.

[5] Frances Moore Lappe, Joseph Collins, and David Kinley, Aid as Obstacle: Twenty Questions about our Foreign Aid and the Hungry (San Francisco: Institute for Food and Development Policy, 1980), p. 43.

[6] This is not to suggest that development professionals as a group have totally ignored comparisons of various strategies to determine what works and what does not. But such comparisons are rare, and are hardly ever based on data collected from the field. See Steven H. Arnold, "A Comparative Study of Five European Development Assistance Programs," U.S. Agency for International Development Occasional Paper, No. 4 (Washington, D.C., 1982).

[7] For a review of this work, see Alec Cairncross and Mohinder Puri, (eds.) Employment, Income Distribution and Development Strategy (London: Macmillan Press, 1979).

[8] Elliott R. Morss, "Institutional Destruction Resulting from Donor and Project Proliferation in Sub-Saharan African Countries," World Development, Vol. 12, no.4 (April 1984), pp. 465-470.

[9] One of the first well-documented statements of dissatisfaction with the "new" approaches concerned Africa. See, World Bank, Accelerated Development in Sub-Saharan Africa: An Agenda for Action (Washington, D.C., 1981).

[10] However, for one of the rare examples of written work on this matter, see Michael Crosswell, "Growth, Poverty Alleviation, and Foreign Assisstance," U.S. Agency for

International Development Discussion Paper, No. 39
(Washington, D.C., 1981).
[11]  See Massachusetts Institute of Technology, Center for
International Studies, "The Objectives of U.S. Econonomic
Assistance Programs."
[12]  See Richard Newfarmer, "A Look at Reagan's Revolution
in Development Policy," Challenge (September/October
1983), pp. 34-43.
[13]  See U.S. Department of State, Report of the Carlucci
Commission on Security and Economic Assistance
(Washington, D.C.: Government Printing Office, 1985).
[14]  See Morawetz, Twenty-Five Years.
[15]  See Charles Murray, Losing Ground: American Social
Policy 1950 - 1980 (New York: Basic Books, 1984).
[16]  For a plan on how to effect the needed changes, see
chapter 7.
[17]  Admittedly, GNP per capita is far from a perfect
normative statistic: in addition to questions that can be
raised about the utility of any purely economic measure,
there is the further point that severe and large pockets
of poverty exist in many nations with incomes in excess of
the $850 number.
[18]  Because of overlaps, there are less than twenty
countries. That is, some countries ranked in the top ten
on both measures.

# 4

---

# The Future: Changes in
# the World Setting

For several decades experts from a panoply of
disciplines have predicted global disaster: a future in
which the basic amenities would not be available to most
people; a world where the present disparities between rich
and poor nations will continue; a global setting fraught
with international violence, nuclear proliferation,
ecological degradation, pollution, and increasing
indebtedness.  Others claim these predictions are "biased,
misleading, and sometimes plain wrong;" that such gloomy,
pessimistic reports with their dour projections reflect
western middle-class perceptions more than a realistic
appraisal of global circumstances.  But the protagonists
concur about one sobering statistic: hundreds of millions
of people live in desperately poor societies which are
unlikely to improve substantially in the near future.  In
fact, no one takes serious issue with the view that the
world faces enormous difficulties in trying to insure
adequate distribution mechanisms for food, shelter,
health, and self-respect for all peoples.  Disagreement
does exist regarding such issues as the magnitude of the
problem, what to do about it, and how to predict future
needs.  Further questions remain unanswered such as what
are the consequences of disruptions in labor markets,
population growth, alternative investment strategies,
ostensible disintegration of life support systems,
changing and even forced migration patterns, technological
advances, and trading restrictions?
    The problem has been that predictions and assumptions
about future national objectives, goals, and changes in
international economic and political postures have been
incomplete.  It is relatively easy to review historical
events about what happened where and when; it is more

difficult to make this jumble of events intelligible to
determine why things happened. Attempts to predict the
future are even more precarious.

The first three chapters reviewed major changes that
have occurred since the initiation of western development
assistance thirty years ago. They described what happened
to developed countries and how their relative economic
positions have changed, and examined the experiences of
developing countries and how a significant portion of them
have become powerful and self-sufficient economic entities
in their own right. Finally, they summarized the changes
that have taken place in development thinking and
critiqued the major donor-sponsored development
initiatives of the last two decades.

This chapter and the following chapters look to the
future and pose questions and issues that need to be
addressed but are often overlooked. Changes in both the
developed and developing world will continue. Some of
these changes can and should be anticipated in any attempt
to define the appropriate future role of western
development assistance. Others are less easy to predict.
These chapters will examine the criteria donors use in
allocating development assistance among nations and
activities. While recognizing the difficulty of
predictions, a number of hypotheses will be offered
regarding future development assistance needs. The
objective here is not as much to be right as to get
western policy makers to see the importance of dealing
with rapid global changes in formulating appropriate
development assistance programs for the future.


FLUCTUATIONS IN THE WORLD SETTING

Substantial changes in global economic circumstances
will significantly affect the prospects of developing
countries over the next decade. If the past can provide
any guidelines for the future, these changes will probably
be more important than anything donors or developing
countries can do to influence economic and social
development. Remarkably, donors have given little
attention to many of these matters, while other problems
have been extensively analyzed and blamed for development
failures.

Looking to the recent past, it is clear that nobody
accurately anticipated the importance of oil price
fluctuations, the micro-electronics revolution, or the

imprudence of international banks in lending to Latin
American countries.  Uncertainty regarding these issues
will continue.  Important current issues with
unpredictable outcomes include the effect of measures to
control the United States government deficit and the
consequences for world aggregate demand as well as the
value of the dollar.  And other unforeseeable events are
likely.

While donors and developing countries have little
control over or ability to predict many of these events,
it is important to recognize that they will influence the
chances for success of most development efforts.  And
alternatives chosen are likely to have profound
consequences in terms of efficiency, production, and
employment.  But what can be done, given world
uncertainties?  A quote from one development expert offers
the proper philosophic starting point:

> we continue to know several things from undeniable
> experience: that our predictive abilities are
> mightily limited; that fortuity is often the most
> potent ingredient in our recipes of action; that
> outcomes frequently depend on the on-the-scene
> ability (and luck) to grasp and exploit fortuitous
> events; and that in sum our plans, proposals, and
> projected solutions are exercises in hopeful
> gaming more than anything else.[1]

Options must be considered in light of the risks and
costs associated with them.  For example, it is not clear
what will happen to oil prices over the next decade.  If
one moves ahead on an initiative that has a significant
impact on oil consumption, one should consider the costs
and benefits of using different oil pricing assumptions.
At the very least, nearly all initiatives should be
subjected to at least some sensitivity testing with the
aim of minimizing the costs associated with the actual
occurence of important, low-probability events.

## INTERDEPENDENCE OF NATIONS

With the costs and barriers associated with
international information transfers falling, financial and
trade flows have grown.  This is increasing the
interdependence among nations, thereby opening the door
for greater competition.  In the presence of free trade
and full capacity utilization, greater competition should

move countries to activities in which they have
comparative advantage, leading in theory to a maximization
of world output. However, leaders of nations are not
nearly as enthusiastic about such an outcome as they might
have been in earlier days. There are good reasons for
this dampened enthusiasm:

1. Greater global interdependence reduces a
   nation's ability to isolate itself from the
   negative effects of external events which it
   can not control, such as oil price changes.

2. Currently, the world is operating at
   considerably less than full capacity
   utilization.

3. Both of the above provide nations with reasons
   to create barriers to trade that will protect
   or augment domestic employment levels and
   cushion their economies from external events.

When the world economy is at or near full capacity
production, the neoclassical theory of comparative
advantage should apply: countries should produce only
those products in which they have a comparative advantage
leaving other forms of production to other nations. So,
for example, during the 1960s and 1970s Japan permitted
other countries in Asia to begin production in certain
industries in which Japan had an absolute advantage. All
this has now changed. The world is no longer at or even
near full employment or capacity production. So long as
this situation continues, nations will compete in
international markets for employment opportunities. In
these circumstances, the system of free trade collapses
and the law of comparative advantage will not drive policy
choices. Moreover, it is reasonable to assume national
policies will be created to establish barriers to trade,
protect or augment domestic employment levels, and in
general cushion local economies from external events.

While there is widespread agreement regarding the
growing importance of economic linkages among nations,
these linkages are complex and hard to model
quantitatively for predictive purposes. One estimate is
that a 1 percent increase in U.S. spending would directly
increase U.S. imports by $1.5 billion within six months.[2]
It has also been estimated that a 1 percent increase in
world demand will cause reductions in unemployment among

European nations of anywhere from 1 to 30 percent.[3]  Most likely reductions in unemployment of similar magnitudes would follow in developing countries.  A recent survey at the World Bank found:

1. A one percent increase in western economic production should increase the demand for developing country exports by something between one and two percent.

2. A depreciation of the U.S. dollar by 10 percent should add somewhat more than 5 percentage points to the growth in real commodity prices over a two year period.

3. A rise in short-term real interest rates increases developing country debt service burdens.[4]

Another study has stressed the importance for global well-being of the path taken to reduce the U.S. trade deficit.[5]  For example, while this investigation agreed that the U.S. government deficit should be reduced, it also recognized that this should be done gradually in coordination with other OECD country policies to minimize the negative effect on developing country exports.

The point here is that economic linkages exist between developed and developing nations, and that probably the most effective actions western nations could take to put the developing world on a sustainable development path have as much to do with increasing the demand for developing country exports through expansionary (and coordinated) monetary and fiscal policies as with reforms in western development assistance programs.

FUTURE UNEMPLOYMENT SCENARIOS

The paragraphs above have emphasized the need to view development assistance from a global perspective and the uncertainties associated with any such look into the future.  This section will put together various pieces of information to develop a scenario which is plausible enough and sufficiently troubling to warrant far more attention than it has received.

Specifically, a case will be made that suggests the Third World will face a massive growth in unemployment over the next decade unless actions are taken to alter

current trends.  But before presenting data to document
that this is plausible, a qualification is in order.  Over
the last two hundred years, there have been repeated
instances in which straight-line or more sophisticated
projections have suggested that massive increases in
unemployment were just over the horizon.  These dire
predictions usually followed some important technological
development, such as the industrial revolution or assembly
line production.  In nearly all cases, these pessimistic
views were based on the single, recurring fear that
machines would take the place of human labor in
production.  Of course, with hindsight, the concern was
unfounded: massive unemployment did not occur.  And
indeed, the most important result of technological
innovations was to increase per capita incomes - a
derivative of the fact that machines made laborers more
productive.  It is in full recognitions of these earlier,
erroneous prognostications that the scenario presented
below is developed.  Certainly, with the facts at hand,
there is a far greater chance that unemployment presents a
major threat than it did in earlier years.  Each of the
major factors contributing to the scenario are presented
and discussed: the micro-electronic revolution, other new
technologies, world food surpluses, non-food commodities,
the debt problem, population growth, and ecological
degradation.

## The Micro-electronic Revolution

Innovations in micro-electronics will undoubtedly
have as profound an influence on labor displacement and
increased productivity as the introduction of mass
production technologies had in the nineteenth century.
How far this labor displacement will go is conjecture.
Nobody disputes the fact that the immediate impact will be
to displace workers; rather, the debate focuses on how
many new jobs will be created in various capital goods,
software, and service industries to complement and
supplement the introduction of the new micro-electronic
technologies.  Further, there is little debate about the
sorts of workers demanded by these new activities: they
will need to be skilled.
For developing countries, the revolution has a very
clear and troubling significance: it will reduce the
competitive advantage they derive from their low-cost,
unskilled labor.  The only developing countries likely to
do well are those with a skilled labor force.  And even

for those countries, one sees some slackening in demand as
plants in Third World countries are closing and moving
back to the United States, Japan, and other technically
advanced nations.   One reason this is happening is
automation destroyed their comparative advantage.
Unfortunately for the developing world, micro-electronic
technologies are being applied in labor-intensive
industries such as the textile industry.   Whereas in the
past, these industries required a well-managed,
inexpensive labor pool but little capital, the new
industries will require large capital investments and
highly skilled laborers.   Other reasons factories are
moving back to industrialized countries are to avoid trade
barriers, transportation costs, and security problems.

It is still too early to accurately project the long-
term effects of these technological innovations.   It is
also too early to predict how rapidly they will be
adopted.   But there can be little question that they will
significantly displace a large number of low-skilled
workers in developing countries.

World Food Surpluses

The world is now producing more food than most
pundits ever imagined possible: numerous countries that
were importing vast stocks of food staples just years ago
are today self-sufficient.   The statistics are startling.
Between 1972 and 1982 farmers in the U.S. increased
agricultural output by 33 percent.   During that same
period agricultural production rose 38 percent in South
America and per capita food production increased 10.5
percent.   In the Philippines increases were 50 percent and
20 percent; in Pakistan they were 36 percent and 5
percent, respectively.   Pakistan is now self-sufficient in
cereals.   Since 1970 wheat production in India has more
than doubled; rice production has expanded 30 percent.
Indonesia used to import one to two million tons of rice a
year; today local production is ample. Other Asia
countries such as Japan, the Philippines, and Taiwan are
producing rice surpluses.   Since China broke up communal
farms and leased the land to families and small groups,
agricultural production has increased 40 percent, prices
paid to farmers increased 25 percent, and the country is
now self-sufficient in grain.   In 1984 the wheat crop in
the European Community was 23 percent higher than ever
previously recorded.   Production of cereals, wheat, rice,
and grains - the staples of world food consumption -

increased 8.5 percent in 1985 over the previous year.
Developing nations as a whole experienced per capita
increases in food production for the fifth consecutive
year, outstripping population growth. In short, the world
has more food than it can absorb.[6]

These remarkable increases in agricultural production
are principally the result of misguided western
agricultural policies and technological developments.
There is every indication that western policies protecting
national farmers and creating incentives for them to
produce more than is demanded will continue. It seems
equally certain that new applications of biogentics and
other technological innovations will continue and even
accelerate. In the United States alone, the Patent and
Trademark Office in the Commerce Department received 5,500
patent applications and issued 850 new patents in the
biotechnology field in 1985. Over the last several years
the Department of Agriculture financed nearly 800
biotechnology research projects, and both commercial and
governmental organizations have invested hundreds of
millions of dollars on experiments and new products. Some
of these products are nearly ready to be marketed. One
company is on the verge of developing a gene that could be
attached to existing genetic structures of plants such as
tomatoes, corn, tobacco, and cotton making them resistant
to certain herbicides. Other research has concentrated on
new plants that would be able to resist drought, salt
water, and metallic soils.[7] The implications are
profound. The United States will produce 80 mmt. of
surplus grain and oilseed in the 1986-1987 crop season.
That is with 15-20 million hectares of fallow cropland.
The U.S. government will buy and store 150 mmt. of grain,
15 mmt. of soybeans and millions of tons of butter,
cheese, and nonfat dry milk, all of which will cost $30
billion a year. The European Community will spend $4
million to store 20 mmt. excess grain, and millions of
tons of sugar, beef, and dairy products. New corn
varities have extended the corn belt 250 miles toward both
poles.[8] Use of fertilizers has increased, pest control
has improved and is more widely used, new farming systems
and land improvement techniques are being adapted,
preventative measures against soil erosion are being
employed, and investment in agricultural research, both
private and public, is sharply escalating. During the
1970s government spending in developing nations on
agricultural research tripled, exceeding the combined
public expenditures in Canada and the United States.[9]

Even in Africa, where traditional farming practices are
the norm and only about one-half of the arable land is
cultivated annually, experts estimate new drought-
resistant seeds and rotational grazing practices could
sharply increase food production.  Fast growing, deep-
rooted leguminous trees could prevent such extensive soil
erosion and deforestation; and improvements in national
agricultural pricing policies and institutional efficiency
could increase small farmer access to new technological
packages and provide incentives to plant more crops.

These figures defy the widely publicized views of
environmentalists regarding the nature and level of hunger
in the world today.  They contend agricultural research
will soon approach diminishing returns, environmental
deterioration will continue, food production systems will
break down resulting in famine and malnutrition affecting
millions of people.  It is more likely that in the year
2000 people will be better fed than is the case today,
despite climatic vagaries and inept government
agricultural policies in many countries.  This is not to
deny the existence of a serious food problem.  However,
the problem does not stem from inadequate food supplies;
rather, hunger and malnutrition in pockets of the globe
are the result of distributional problems, the lack of
purchasing power, and poor sanitary and health conditions.
Many deaths in Third World countries attributed to hunger
are probably due to other problems such as lack of potable
water, diarrhetic diseases, and inadequate medical
treatment.  Serious malnutrition, it is estimated, affects
only about 6 percent of the world's population.[10]

Understandably, the question of food security is
basic to the welfare of citizens of any nation.  The
appropriate policies to achieve this status and the
implications for employment generation are more
problematic.  In many developing countries the major
source of employment has been and continues to be in the
agricultural sector.  There are a number of experts who
argue that, despite increasing global food supplies, the
most sensible growth strategy for a primarily agricultural
developing nation to follow is to expand the agricultural
sector.  The argument is based on the assumption that
surplus agricultural production will be consumed locally,
providing cash for the farmers and saving foreign exchange
that would otherwise be required to import food products.
Excess cash would be invested in small agricultural
industries or non-farm small industries, creating jobs in
rural areas, curtailing urban migration, and developing a

traditional industrial sector to provide capital for the
modern economy.[11]

This is certainly a plausible assumption.  Take the
case of Morocco.  During the 1960s agricultural production
increased on average at 3.6 percent per year, and domestic
production covered 87 percent of cereal needs.  In the
1970s and 1980s the average annual growth rate in the
agricultural sector was down to 1.2 percent per year.
Between 1980 and 1983 domestic production covered only 62
percent of cereal needs.  This country had a surplus
balance of trade in agricultural commodities in 1974: that
had turned into a deficit of $375 million by 1984.  Today
about one-third of the poorest 45 percent of Moroccan
families spend over 80 percent of their household income
on food.  While agricultural production decreased
population increased.  At the current growth rate of 2.7
percent annually the population of Morocco will double by
2012, and it is estimated that the economy will only be
able to generate around two-thirds of the jobs required to
absorb the annual net new employees in the labor force.

This combination of problems - decreasing food
production and agricultural exports, increasing population
and unemployment - has led donor agencies to support
extensive projects to increase agricultural production.[12]
There is, however, another side to the equation.  From a
global standpoint food adequacy is not a problem.  It is
more realistic to view the world as producing far more
food than it needs largely because western farm policies
are generating the wrong incentives.  The current world
food "glut" has troubling implications for rural
employment in developing countries.  Food prices are
likely to continue to fall in real terms.  In addition, it
is likely that most of the technological advances will
favor the high input production modes of the West, thereby
worsening the competitive position of developing
countries.  This raises serious questions about the
capacity of developing countries to be competitive in
world food markets.

## Non-Food Commodities

In 1976 the Club of Rome predicted a severe shortage
in virtually all raw materials by 1985.[13]  Not only have
these shortages failed to materialize, but as Peter
Drucker has noted raw materials are at their lowest levels
in recorded history relative to the prices of manufactured
goods and services.[14]  This fall in commodity prices stems

from a reduction in demand. A recent International
Monetary Fund study shows that since 1900, the use of raw
materials per unit of economic output have fallen on
average by 1.25 percent annually.[15]

In looking to the future, one needs to know the
reasons for this reduction in demand and use in order to
speculate sensibly on whether they will continue. It
appears that the primary source of the fall in demand has
been the introduction of new production technologies.
These technologies have either reduced the amount of
material needed per unit output or have found a less
expensive material substitute. For example, Japan in 1984
used per unit output only 60 percent of the raw materials
it used in 1973. Drucker offers another striking example
of what is happening: 100 pounds of fiberglass cable
transmit as many telephone messages as does one ton of
copper wire. In this case, sand is being substituted for
copper as the raw material in use.

Can this reduction in demand be expected to continue?
After reviewing a wide range of applications including
those in the energy industry, Drucker concludes:

> ...it is unlikely that raw material prices will
> ever rise substantially as compared to the prices
> of manufactured goods (or high-knowledge services
> such as information, education, or health care)
> except in the event of a major prolonged war.

Drucker might be right: his arguments do sound
plausible. However, one can also point to the fact that
ultimately, the supplies of certain raw materials are
finite and that as a result, a point will be reached at
which prices will escalate sharply as the supply of the
material dries up. Certainly, this was the thinking
underlying the Club of Rome report and the Global 2000
report.[16]

Our view is that Drucker is closer to being right
than those who worry about the exhaustion of raw
materials. It appears that when raw material prices
escalate, new technologies develop quite rapidly to reduce
demand. Often, this does not happen in a smooth fashion -
witness oil price fluctuations - but it seems to be
happening in a sufficiently regular and pervasive fashion
to suggest that employment prospects in raw material
industries will continue to fall for the foreseeable
future.

In short, primary products - agricultural, minerals
and metals - are less and less important to the

development of industrialized nations. A consequence for
Third World countries is that the market for many primary
goods is likely to be depressed. The direct effect on
employment for some agricultural products such as sugar,
oil seeds, and rice could be severe as new technologies
almost eliminate the significance of inexpensive labor and
land as inputs. For the production of mineral products
such as copper, aluminium, and oil it is the indirect
effect of declining foreign exchange earnings that
matters. But both effects are already being felt in a
number of developing countries: new technologies are
already and will probably continue to significantly reduce
the economic advantage of producing in many developing
nations.

## The Debt Service Burden

During the 'seventies, the leading international
banks received large new deposits from oil-exporting
countries. A considerable portion of this buildup in
assets was lent to a number of middle-income countries,
including a handful located in Latin America. The
decisions to make these loans were not based on the cash
flow assessments usually employed by banks, nor were they
based on macro assessments of the recipients ability to
repay the loans, but rather upon a guarantee from the
government of the borrowing country that the loans would
be repaid on schedule.

In retrospect, these lending decisions appear to have
been extremely imprudent. Many countries have been unable
to repay their loans on schedule, and for a period of
time, there was a real chance a number of the major banks
would be forced into bankruptcy. In 1982 the exposure of
the twenty-four largest U.S. banks to oil-importing
developing countries as measured by the claims to capital
ratio reached 200 percent.[17]

The major banks opposed any loan defaults because
of the effects they would have on their balance sheets and
negotiated reductions of current debt service charges,
extensions of maturity periods, and some reductions in
debt charges. Between 1975 and 1985 the World Bank
estimates that 144 renegotiations took place that involved
$205 billion in loans.

An element in virtually every renegotiation agreement
was a promise by the borrowing government to take steps to
improve its international merchandise trade account so as
to be in a better position to make debt service payments

in hard currencies.  The primary means of doing this was
to reduce domestic aggregate demand through such measures
as tighter monetary and fiscal policies.  An unfortunate
by-product of these actions is a lessening of domestic
economic activity, thereby increasing unemployment.  In
short, at a time when growing unemployment constitutes a
serious problem, developing countries are being required
by their creditors to take actions that will contribute
further to unemployment levels.  For most countries, it is
unlikely that these requirements will be removed in the
near future as a result of the lengthening of the debt
payments schedule.
     While the debt problems of Latin America have
received most of the attention, debt servicing has become
a serious problem for most developing nations.  Table 4.1
presents two commonly used debt burden indicators for
developing country groups.  One weakness of the ratios
presented in table 4.1 is their static nature.
Recognition of the severity of the problem

Table 4.1
Debt Service Burdens for Developing Countries, 1984
(In percentages)

| Country Group | Debt Service to Export Ratio | Debt Service to GNP Ratio |
|---|---|---|
| Low Income African | 14.9 | 2.5 |
| Low Income Asian | 13.3 | 1.2 |
| Middle Income Oil Importers | 16.7 | 4.7 |
| Oil Exporters | 22.0 | 5.8 |
| Major Borrowers | 20.5 | 4.3 |

Source: World Bank, Development and Debt Service
(Washington, D.C., 1986).

comes from noting that the debt service charges for sub-
Saharan Africa will increase from a 1982-1984 average of
$5.9 billion to a 1985-1987 average of $10.7 billion.  It
is also worth remembering that oil-exporting nations
operate under the largest debt service burdens.  With the
exception of Mexico, these burdens have not caused them
serious problems to date.  However, if oil prices remain
at their current low prices, these countries will be

forced to cutback on expenditures which, among other
things, will eliminate many jobs for workers from other
developing nations.

Regarding the Latin American debt crisis, it should
be recognized that the crisis would never have happened if
the large, western, commercial banks had not made a number
of foolish loans during the 'seventies. Rather than
carefully reviewing each loan application, they put on
blinders and, in their effort to move a lot of money in a
hurry, made loans whenever they could obtain a guarantee
from the government of the recipient nation. It is
consistent with the spirit of our free enterprise
philosophy to let the banks suffer the consequences of
these actions. Unfortunately, too much is at stake in
this instance to look the other way. As a consequence,
western nations are pushing additional monies out through
the International Monetary Fund, the World Bank, and the
bilateral aid programs to bail the banks out. This is an
inefficient way to deal with the crisis. Moreover, it
diverts attention from the banks that made these loans in
the first place and to the recipient nations. A more
attractive solution would be to allow the commercial banks
to use these debt certificates as collateral to obtain
funding from their central bank. It should be understood
that these loans would be provided so that the banks could
relax the terms of repayment, thereby reducing the extent
of the debt crisis. The central bank should require that
the commercial banks reduce their loans as debt service
payments are received from the debtor countries. The
advantage of this approach is that it focuses attention on
the commercial banks and requires them to borrow for past
mistakes.

## Ecological Concerns

Recent famines in Africa and Asia have raised western
sensitivity to the plight of millions of people who barely
subsist. By and large these people live in peasant
economies based on the production of renewable or
nonrenewable natural resources. And there is no question
ecological systems are breaking down in many of these
Third World countries. Ecologists have claimed that
alterations and stresses from increasing demand on some
ecosystems are severe enough that the ecosystem will
continually deteriorate and eventually collapse.
Perpetual overuse of biological systems, they argue,
creates a chain reaction of deterioration with each

disruption of the natural balance causing further
adjustments that may eventually result in complete
instability. The cycle works like this: Increasing
population requires additional land for production and
household fuels; forests and woodlands are cleared for
crops, livestock, and fuel; intensive nonregenerative land
use ensues; vegetation density and soil nutrition are
reduced; as the soil cover deteriorates the capacity to
retain water diminishes; rainfall runs off; soil erosion
increases; people seek new virgin territory to clear; and,
unless the cycle is broken, human demands will exceed the
capacity of the biological systems.

Consider the evidence. According to a survey of
ecological trends between 1977-1985 of twenty countries in
Africa, not one of the indicators of ecological
deterioration (sand dune encroachment, rangeland
deterioration, forest depletion, decline of irrigation
systems, and rain-fed agricultural systems) showed
improvement. One observer of the complex connections and
interactions in ecosystems commented that it is likely
there will not be enough water in the lake above the
Panama Canal to operate the locks in twenty years because
rapid deforestation of the watershed that feeds the lake
is causing siltation.[18] And these are not isolated
examples.

Development planners have been accused of overlooking
ecological concepts and the biological carrying capacity
of the world. As a result of this oversight, some experts
argue world demand for food and fuel has stretched and
weakened natural systems, presaging a gradual economic
decline, social fragmentation, and the break down of
political structures.[19] Undoubtedly, environmental
degradation exists: topsoil is eroding, tropical forests
are disappearing, and nonrenewable resources are
declining. The issue is are development experts asking
the right questions about the consequences of tampering
with the environment, and are governments prepared to make
unpopular, political and economic decisions about land
use?

Population Growth

World population increased by about 80 million people
in 1984; most of this increase was in Third World
countries where two-thirds of the world's population live.
Since World War II growth rates in developing nations have
been averaging between 2 and 4 percent per year. This

level is unprecedented and has placed an enormous burden
on agrarian countries that have insufficient human and
physical capital, inadequate political and social
institutions, and little unused land.

Many of the current industrialized nations
experienced rapid growth and structural transformation in
the nineteenth century, but that is where the comparison
to the growth occurring in developing nations today ends.
The large shift of labor from agricultural work to
industries and services was possible in the nineteenth
century because technologies were less advanced. Rural
workers did not need to be well educated to work in these
industries. Furthermore, technological advances did not
displace labor as they often do today. There were vast
tracts of unused land and opportunities to emigrate, so
pressure on the land was not as great as it is today.[20]

As the World Bank has pointed out, aggregate global
population escalation in the future may strain world
resources:

> But for the next five or six decades, the problem
> goes beyond one of global resources and is less
> easily amenable to any technological fix. It is a
> mismatch between population and income-producing
> ability, a mismatch that leaves many of the
> world's people in a vicious circle of poverty and
> high fertility.[21]

If a country has a population growth rate of between
2 and 4 percent per year, about 40 percent of the
population will be under 15 years of age. Even if
fertility rates decrease substantially population growth
will continue well into the twenty-first century,
requiring the creation of new jobs for an expanding labor
force and additional food supplies. The working age
population in Columbia, for example, will rise from 15
million in 1980 to 25 million in 2000; in Bangladesh it
will almost double from 48 to 84 million over the same
period.[22]

In order to maintain current productivity and income
in countries where there is a growing labor force, i.e.,
most Third World nations, capital investment should grow
faster than the labor force. This means accelerated
government investment in education, health systems,
infrastructure, agricultural equipment and research, and
industrial facilities. In many developing countries
sufficient resources are simply not available or trade-

offs are made in favor of additional short-term consumption. So despite rapid expansion of education systems and other capital investments, the number of illiterate and poorly educated workers is actually greater now in some countries than it was twenty years ago.

## Some Reflections on Future Global Unemployment

How seriously should this unemployment scenario be taken, and what are the implications for developing nations? While we believe it is certainly plausible enough to be taken seriously, but there are probably three or four alternative scenarios that also warrant careful scrutiny. The primary implication of the unemployment scenario for all nations is that they will be forced to compete for job-generating goods and service industries. Market access will continue to be the most important factor in the decision where to locate an industry or service, so countries with large domestic markets will not have to "bid" as much for job-generating activities as nations with smaller domestic markets. "Bids" will likely include various types of cost-reducing items, such as subsidized labor, tax holidays, and lower-than-market rental space. In the immediate future this bidding activity will result in a transfer of resources from nations to organizations with employment opportunities to "sell." In other words, so long as unemployment rates are high, transnational corporations will be in a position to negotiate advantageous terms with Third World countries prior to locating a plant there. This "sellers market" will continue until something approximating an equilibrium between supply and demand is achieved in world labor markets.

## THE ADEQUACY OF DEVELOPMENT ECONOMICS

In recent years, a number of senior development economists have asserted that their profession has not lived up to expectations. These mea culpas have taken various forms. One group believes projections were overly optimistic regarding how long it would take and how difficult it would be to launch developing countries on sustainable growth paths.[23] Another group appears to have been "in the trenches" too long. Expressing frustration and exhaustion with past efforts, these experts are exhibiting all the signs of intellectual "burn-out."[24] There is a final group looking for new approaches and modes of analysis of which perhaps the most thoughtful piece has been done by Bruton.[25] He asserts that failures have occurred, and will continue to occur so long as we attempt to impose western values, processes, and systems on developing nations: developing nations must themselves "search, learn and choose" to find their own ways. He concedes that this will be difficult, given the temptations and pressures to copy the approaches of wealthy western nations.

A number of observations are in order. The progress of developing countries as measured by western economic and social indicators has been quite remarkable over the last several decades.[26] Indeed, a major reason for rethinking the consequences of western assistance is that a number of developing countries have emerged as major competitors of western nations.

Most development economists would concede this point; some are more concerned with other quality of life dimensions. For example, Bruton is hopeful developing countries can find approaches of their own and in so doing avoid the tensions, disappointments, and resentments that result from adopting the western approach. In passing, it is worth noting that western development was not a painless process: the industrial revolution was a period of great hardship, tension, and exploitation. The question, and it is not a new question, is whether there are other models worth considering. As historical empiricists, we are skeptical of finding workable alternatives. But even if they could be developed, it is highly unlikely western experts, imbued as they are with their own values and sense of history, will make much of a contribution to these new approaches.

In our view, western development advisors could better spend their time revising their own models and analytical techniques to reflect changing world conditions. The changes that need to be allowed for have already been mentioned above. They include:

1. increasing uncertainty regarding world developments;

2. international prices that do not reflect costs;

3. the growing oligopolistic nature of world markets;

4. the accelerated pace of economic activity; and

5. a continuation of high unemployment rates.

Taken together, these changes mean the methods traditionally used by development economists are simply too cumbersome to be useful.

Consider the tools used to predict the consequences of an investment. Economists have traditionally used benefit/cost or some other form of rate of return technique to determine the attractiveness of alternative investments. In using these techniques, they make point estimates of various future prices and costs. For example, many important investment decisions were made on the basis of assumptions regarding future oil prices. In retrospect, most of these assumptions were incorrect. The difficulty of making accurate predictions is important information and should be factored into current analytical work.

There is considerable evidence that international prices deviate significantly from production costs. This is best documented in the agricultural field where western nations heavily subsidize the industry and developing countries exploit it.[27] It is also obvious in the oil industry where the strength of the oil cartel has been a more important determinant of oil prices than anything having to do with production costs. Increasingly, international procurement involves some sort of countertrade agreement which brings into further question what prices actually reflect. And finally, the various preferential treatment agreements allow a wide variety of goods to be sold at different international prices.

More and more international markets are providing evidence of oligopolistic behavior. This provides further documentation that market prices do not reflect production costs. But in addition, oligopolistic behavior makes strategic decision making more complex. Specifically, it means that in addition to making the usual marketing and cost calculations, one must also anticipate how other sellers will react to any actions one takes. So, for example, if a sub-Saharan African nation is considering an effort to regain its market share in a particular crop, it must look not only at existing world prices and costs, but also, it must anticipate how other countries will react to its attempt to increase market share, e.g., how would Brazil react to a Ghanaian attempt to regain its share of the cocoa market? Of course, these considerations soon become exceedingly complex.

It used to be that a country could attempt to
establish a new agricultural or industrial base at a
leisurely pace. This is no longer the case. Improved
information technologies plus an acceleration in the pace
of technological advancement has changed this. The micro-
electronics field is perhaps at one extreme, but it does
emphasize some major trends: a micro-electronic "chip" has
an expected market life of eighteen months and an initial
investment requirement of $200 million.[28] A decade ago, a
number of American companies moved their production to
Asia to take advantage of low cost, skilled labor. As
indicated earlier, this production is now returning to the
United States because the micro-electronics revolution is
rapidly diminishing the importance of the labor input.
The point is the rapidity with which change is taking
place. One can't help wondering what chance a country not
used to such a pace has of ever competing in international
markets.

Most western models and analytic methods presume a
world in which there is a tendency toward full employment
and prices largely reflect the opportunity costs of
production. As was discussed above, there are good
reasons to question this presumption, certainly over the
short- to medium-term. In the absence of a movement to
full employment, comparative advantage provides little
guidance as to what a country should produce. This is
because in the absence of full employment, countries with
an absolute advantage in the production of good X will not
be willing to cede its production to another country just
because the latter has the comparative advantage.

In short, there are numerous reasons to question the
adequacy of the tools used by development economists to
deal with issues of international trade and development in
a western world system. Below, we offer a preliminary
outline of what is needed to make the profession more
useful and relevant.

Taking a global perspective, the development
economists should continually emphasize how difficult
things become when world economic activity is at a level
significantly below full capacity utilization. They
should urge western countries and emerging nations to
adopt coordinated policies to achieve full capacity
utilization. The United States is no longer large enough
to effect this goal by itself. Indeed, with a merchandise
trade deficit now approaching $200 billion, many would
argue it is doing far more than it should to stimulate
world demand.

They should also emphasize the importance of curbing population growth rates in those developing countries that have not "emerged". As will be discussed in chapter 6, effective steps to reduce population growth are probably more important for the development of these countries than are their other economic policies.

Development economists must also be willing to accept reality and incorporate uncertainty into their analysis. Precisely what needs to be done here will take more work. A start would be to engage in sensitivity testing on key variables, and from this develop loss and benefit functions for alternative scenarios.[29] In this regard, finding a way to identify a complete plausible scenario is far more important than working out detailed policy recommendations for a particular scenario. When this has been done and uncertainty concerning the proper course remains "hedging" strategies should be developed to allow a country to keep its options open until more information is available.

When working on the development strategy for a particular country, the economist should be willing to put on "partial equilibrium blinders" and focus exclusively on what serves the interests of the country. While on the face of it, this might seem to be an exercise of limited intellectual interest, the reality is that given the growing complexity of the world situation, its uncertainty, and rapidity of change, this task, if properly done, should present a most significant intellectual challenge.

The development economist must be willing to get into far greater detail that was true in the past. If the job is being properly done, one soon moves beyond policy recommendations such as "liberalization," "labor intensive," and "outward looking." Based upon a limited number of artificial exercises of the sort being proposed here, it is likely that one will end up recommending to protect certain industries (more accurately, to protect jobs) from outside competition and to subsidize or protect other industries in hopes of breaking into certain export markets. In addition, there are likely to be special "deals" worth negotiating. For example, it was recently learned that a U.S. company sold fighter planes to Turkey and in exchange agreed to sell Turkish agricultural products to Eastern bloc countries.

New types of information will have to be assembled and analyzed: it is no longer adequate to talk in general terms about cost structures of industries. Now it is necessary to have detailed cost data by industry and to consider whether and/or how long potential or actual competitors would be willing to produce at a loss to prevent a country or firm from increasing its market share.

In sum, it would appear that the western development economist faces a formidable but challenging task. Western approaches do not appear to be so much to blame as the reluctance of their users to adapt their models and analytical techniques to a rapidly changing world.

SUMMARY

There is great uncertainty on how the issues discussed above will be resolved, or what new issues will emerge.

How, for example, will oil prices move during the next two decades? Will there continue to be major, unanticipated swings as has been the pattern since 1972, or will they move higher gradually as a reflection of the dwindling stocks of world oil supplies?

Concerning world food supplies, are China and Russia likely to stabilize their production at higher levels thereby contributing to existing food surpluses?

How fast will the new biogenetic discoveries be introduced and how will they effect production?

Will there be a smooth transition through the debt crisis, or will one of the less desirable scenarios occur?

Will the world continue its move back towards full capacity utilization and thereby dampen current pressures for increased trade restrictions?

How fast will the new production methods relying on micro-electronics be introduced?

Has inattentive land-use management resulted in irreversible damage to large areas in Third World nations?

Putting these strands together, there is growing evidence to support a serious concern about a potential unemployment crisis in developing countries: the global food surplus, the micro-electronics revolution, continuing population growth, the fall in oil prices, and questions regarding western nations ability to increase world aggregate demand all contribute to this.

NOTES

[1]  William J. Siffin, "Administrative Problems and Integrated Rural Development," A PASITAM Design Study (Bloomington: Indiana University, 1979), p.2.
[2]  Ray Fair, "Estimated Output, Price, Interest Rate, and Exchange Rate Linkages Among Countries," Journal of Political Economy, 90 (June 1982), pp. 507-535.
[3]  See James E. Alt, "Political Parties, World Demand, and Unemployment," American Political Science Review, 79 (December 1985), pp. 1016-1040.
[4]  Rudiger Dornbusch, "The Effects of OECD Macroeconomic Policies on Non-Oil Developing Countries: A Review," World Bank Working Paper, No. 793 (Washington, D.C., 1985).
[5]  Stephen Marris, Deficits and the Dollar: The World Economy at Risk (Washington, D.C.: Institute for International Economics, 1985).
[6]  U.N. World Food Council, Current World Food Situation (Rome, 1985), pp. 1,5,17; Ward Sinclair, "The World Doesn't Need Our Farmers," The Washington Post, December 29, 1985; State Department, Bureau of Intelligence and Research, "Potential for Expanding World Food Production by Region and Country," Report No. 1182-AR (Washington, D.C., October 15, 1985), pp. 1-5,12-15; Dennis Avery, "The New U.S. Farm Law: Challenge - or Retreat?" Remarks at the U.S. Embassy Brussels, Belgium, March 10, 1986, p. 7.
[7]  W. John Moore, "Genes for Sale," National Journal, Vol. 18, no. 25 (1986), p. 1528.
[8]  Dennis Avery, "The New U.S. Farm Law," p. 7; State Department, Bureau of Intelligence and Research, "Potential for Expanding World Food Production," p. 1.
[9]  State Department, Bureau of Intelligence and Research "Potential for Expanding," p. 1.  For an interesting summary of the pioneering work of the thirteen institutions forming the Consultative Group on

International Agricultural Research and their contribution
to agricultural research in developing nations see, State
Department, Bureau of Intelligence and Research, "Food
Production: The Success of the International Agricultural
Research Centers," Report No. 751-AR (Washington, D.C.,
January 4, 1984).

[10] Dennis T. Avery, "Hunger in a World of Plenty," Paper
prepared for the Luthern Hunger Conference, held at Kansas
City, January 30, 1986, p. 1.

[11] See John W. Mellor, "Agriculture on the Road to
Industrialization," Reprint from John P. Lewis and
Valeriana Kallab, (eds.), Development Strategies
Reconsidered (Washington, D.C.: Overseas Development
Council, 1986), chapter 2.

[12] Agency for International Development, "Country
Development Strategy Statement, FY 1988 Morocco,"
(Washington, D.C., February 1986), pp. 13-31.

[13] See Donella H. Meadows et al., The Limits to Growth
(Washington, D.C.: Potomac Associates, 1974).

[14] Peter F. Drucker, "The Changed World Economy," Foreign
Affairs, Vol. 64, no. 4 (Spring 1986), pp. 768-791.

[15] David Sapsford, "Real Commodity Prices: An Analysis of
Long-Run Movements," International Monetary Fund Internal
Memorandum, May 17, 1985.

[16] For the Club of Rome report see, Meadows et al., The
Limits to Growth; also see, Council on Environmental
Quality, The Global 2000 Report to the President of the
United States (New York: Pergamon Press, 1980).

[17] U.S. Federal Financial Institution Examination Council
Release (Washington, D.C., 1985).

[18] Lester R. Brown and Edward C. Wolf, "Assessing
Ecological Decline," in Lester R. Brown et al., (eds.)
State of the World (New York: W.W. Norton & Company,
1986), pp.26-27; Rochelle L. Stanfield, "In the Same
Boat," National Journal, No. 33-34 (August 16, 1986), pp.
1992-1997.

[19] Some proponents of this position contend that the
world is running out of nonrenewable resources based on
the laws of therodynamics; all matter and energy is
constant: it can't be created or destroyed, and moves in
one direction, from usable to unusable. These physical
constraints set limits to human behavior and material
growth. Modern economic theory has never made the
transtion from the concept of infinite material growth to
espousing the conservation of finite resources, proponents
of this position argue. Instead classical economists
believe price mechanisms can prevent problems of scarce
resources. For an explanation of this thesis see, Jeremy
Rifkin, Entropy (New York: The Viking Press, 1980).

20  World Bank, <u>World Development Report 1984</u> (Washington,
D.C., 1984), pp. 60, 79, 88.
21  <u>Ibid</u>, p. 184.
22  <u>Ibid.</u>, pp. 67, 184.
23  For example, see Albert O. Hirschman, "The Rise and
Decline of Development Economics," in Mark Gersovitz,
Carlos F. Diaz-Alejandro, Gustav Ranis and Mark R.
Rosengweig (eds.), <u>The Theory and Experience of Economic
Development</u> (London: George Allen & Unwin, 1982).
24  See John P. Lewis, "Development Promotion: A Time for
Regrouping," in John P. Lewis and Valeriana Kallab (eds.),
<u>Development Strategies Reconsidered</u>, overview.
25  Henry J. Bruton, "The Search for a Development
Economics," <u>World Development</u>, Vol. 13, no. 10/11
(October/November 1985), pp. 1099-1124.
26  For example, see the Development Assistance Committee,
<u>Twenty-Five Years of Development Cooperation: A Review</u>,
(Paris: The Organization for Economic Co-operation and
Development, 1985).
27  World Bank, <u>World Development Report 1986</u> (Washington
D.C., 1986), chapter 1.
28  David Wheeler and Ashoka Mody, "Automation and World
Competition," Report prepared for the Korean Traders
Association (Boston: Boston University, 1986).
29  For at least a start on this matter, see Alexander H.
Sarris and Irma Adelman, "Incorporating Uncertainty into
Planning of Industrialization Strategies for Developing
Countries,"  World Bank Working Paper, No. 503
(Washington, D.C.,1982).

# 5

## Rethinking the Sources and Uses of ODA Monies

As was discussed previously, wealthier developing nations receive more aid on a per capita basis than poorer nations, and aid to Africa is considerably greater per capita than aid to the poorer nations in Asia. This chapter will consider the appropriateness of such distributions, and explore other criteria for future aid contributions.

One may argue that such musings are worthless because when it comes to questions of source and use political considerations of donor nations will determine what is done. Unquestionably, the motivations of donors respecting issues such as national security interests, historical linkages, a substitute for the reduction of trade barriers, and a host of other nation-state concerns will continue to play important roles in determining where aid monies go.[1] Nonetheless, it is valuable to speculate on where aid monies should go in the absence of such provincial concerns. Putting it somewhat more positively, are there global considerations that might offer guidance on aid allocations? One never knows when the opportunities to invoke such criteria will arise, but they frequently do.

CRITERIA FOR ODA CONTRIBUTIONS

For a number of years, the Development Advisory Committee (DAC) of the OECD and others have urged developed countries to make one percent of GNP available as aid. DAC member countries have never come close to achieving this goal: as a group, they have never contributed more than 40 percent of this amount. Turning the matter around, if the 1 percent criterion had been met by OECD nations in 1982, their contribution to ODA would have been $73 billion rather than the actual $28 billion! As this criterion has not been followed it is worth asking whether a more meaningful measure might be found.

Looking at the matter globally, there is some appeal to the argument that the richer countries should do something to help the poorer countries. However, the OECD criterion assumes all "richer" countries are in similar circumstances, and this is most certainly not the case. Two differences are important enough to be worth mentioning. First, there are richer and poorer OECD countries. According to the World Bank, Switzerland had an average per capita income of $17,010 in 1982, while Italy's was only $6,840. Second, the balance of payments circumstances of these countries differ. And here, one can ask whether it is appropriate from a global standpoint for the United States, which is today running a merchandise trade deficit in excess of $100 billion, to be bearing almost as large a share of the ODA burden as it did when it had a positive trade position.

There is, incidentally, evidence that these considerations do play a role in determining ODA contributions of some nations. During and following the oil crisis, the per capita incomes and balance of payments surpluses of the Gulf states became very large. In response, these states greatly expanded their ODA contributions. They have individually given as much as 15.6 percent of GNP (Qatar in 1975). With the falling oil prices of recent years, the contribution of the Gulf states has declined with the result that total ODA has levelled off in 1982 dollars at slightly more than $36 billion.

For illustrative purposes, the implications of using somewhat different criteria for ODA contributions will be considered. The following examples assume the same amount of ODA will be raised in the future as now and will be limited to OECD countries. The first example involves adjusting existing contributions for balance of payments circumstances, where circumstances are defined as the current account balance divided by merchandise exports.[2] The adjustment involves reducing or increasing a country's contribution by this ratio and then adjusting total contributions by a multiple to insure the same ODA is collected. The results are presented in table 5.1.

Table 5.1
ODA Contributions Adjusted for Balance of Payments Circumstances

| Country | 1982 ODA | ODA as percent GNP | ODA Share | Revised 1982 ODA | Percent Change ODA | Revised ODA Share |
|---|---|---|---|---|---|---|
| United States | 8.202 | 0.27 | 29.6 | 7.131 | -13.1 | 25.7 |
| France | 4.034 | 0.75 | 14.5 | 3.298 | -18.2 | 11.9 |
| Germany | 3.152 | 0.48 | 11.4 | 3.829 | 21.5 | 13.8 |
| United Kingdom | 1.800 | 0.37 | 6.5 | 1.904 | 5.8 | 6.9 |
| Netherlands | 1.472 | 1.08 | 5.3 | 1.691 | 14.9 | 6.1 |
| Italy | 0.811 | 0.24 | 2.9 | 0.729 | -10.1 | 2.6 |
| Belgium | 0.501 | 0.59 | 1.8 | 0.486 | -3.0 | 1.8 |
| Denmark | 0.415 | 0.76 | 1.5 | 0.404 | -2.7 | 1.5 |
| Japan | 3.023 | 0.28 | 10.9 | 3.454 | 14.3 | 12.5 |
| Canada | 1.197 | 0.41 | 4.3 | 1.557 | 30.1 | 5.6 |
| Sweden | 0.987 | 1.02 | 3.6 | 1.043 | 5.7 | 3.8 |
| Australia | 0.882 | 0.56 | 3.2 | 0.865 | -1.9 | 3.1 |
| Norway | 0.559 | 0.99 | 2.0 | 0.681 | 21.8 | 2.5 |
| Switzerland | 0.252 | 0.25 | 0.9 | 0.246 | -2.4 | 0.9 |
| Austria | 0.235 | 0.35 | 0.8 | 0.193 | -17.9 | 0.7 |
| Finland | 0.144 | 0.30 | 0.5 | 0.154 | 6.9 | 0.6 |
| New Zealand | 0.065 | 0.28 | 0.2 | 0.067 | 3.1 | 0.2 |
| TOTAL | 27.731 | 0.38 | 100.0 | 27.732 | 0.0 | 100.0 |

Source: OECD, 1984 Review.

As the table indicates, use of this allocation rule would lead to a reduction in the share of eight countries: the United States, France, Italy, Belgium, Denmark, Australia, Switzerland, and Austria. The share of the remaining countries with positive current account balances would be increased.

A second possible criterion would involve two adjustments. The first would be to get all countries to contribute 0.38 percent of their GNP, the current average contribution for all the DAC members of the OECD. This contribution would then be corrected as above for balance of payments circumstances. This criterion maintains the principal that contributions should be some portion of GNP, but with allowance for current contribution levels and with allowance for differing balance of payments circumstances. The results of employing this criterion are presented in table 5.2.

72

Table 5.2
ODA Contributions Adjusted to Same GNP Ratio and for
Balance of Payments Circumstances

| Country | 1982 ODA | ODA as percent GNP | Present ODA Share | Revised 1982 ODA | Percent Change ODA | Revised ODA Share |
|---|---|---|---|---|---|---|
| United States | 8.202 | 0.27 | 29.6 | 10.842 | 32.2 | 39.1 |
| France | 4.034 | 0.75 | 14.5 | 1.146 | -71.6 | 4.1 |
| Germany | 3.152 | 0.48 | 11.4 | 3.130 | -0.7 | 11.3 |
| United Kingdom | 1.800 | 0.37 | 6.5 | 1.969 | 9.4 | 7.1 |
| Netherlands | 1.472 | 1.08 | 5.3 | 0.657 | -55.4 | 2.4 |
| Italy | 0.811 | 0.24 | 2.9 | 1.252 | 54.4 | 4.5 |
| Belgium | 0.501 | 0.59 | 1.8 | 0.294 | -41.3 | 1.1 |
| Denmark | 0.415 | 0.76 | 1.5 | 0.180 | -56.6 | 0.6 |
| Japan | 3.023 | 0.28 | 10.9 | 4.655 | 54.0 | 16.8 |
| Canada | 1.197 | 0.41 | 4.3 | 1.469 | 22.7 | 5.3 |
| Sweden | 0.987 | 1.02 | 3.6 | 0.371 | -62.4 | 1.3 |
| Australia | 0.882 | 0.56 | 3.2 | 0.561 | -36.4 | 2.0 |
| Norway | 0.559 | 0.99 | 2.0 | 0.308 | -44.9 | 1.1 |
| Switzerland | 0.252 | 0.25 | 0.9 | 0.391 | 55.2 | 1.4 |
| Austria | 0.235 | 0.35 | 0.8 | 0.216 | -8.1 | 0.8 |
| Finland | 0.144 | 0.30 | 0.5 | 0.197 | 36.8 | 0.7 |
| New Zealand | 0.065 | 0.28 | 0.2 | 0.093 | 43.1 | 0.3 |
| TOTAL | 27.731 | 0.38 | 100.0 | 27.731 | 0.0 | 100.0 |

Source: OECD, 1984 Review.

Use of this criterion leads to quite different results than in the first example. Most importantly, there are a number of countries, such as the United States, in which the increase in GNP share outweighs the reduction in ODA share resulting from balance of payments problems.

The above examples are presented for illustrative purposes only. While we recommended that the OECD consider alternative guidelines for setting foreign assistance contributions along the lines suggested above, it is not anticipated that OECD nations will agree to any new rules any more than they adhere to the present criteria. But as global circumstances change it is helpful to introduce more flexibility into the inter-country dialogue on development assistance.

CRITERIA FOR ODA USES

The OECD one percent guideline may be thought of as an ODA "supply" statistic. In what follows, attention is given to "demand" or use measures that might be employed in judging whether the geographic allocation of aid monies is appropriate.  Attention will first be given to whether, when viewed from a global standpoint, there is any conceptual justification for one or another use criterion.

Two points come immediately to mind.  First, economic assistance monies constitute public capital.  They are not provided by governments to compete with the domestic and foreign providers of private capital.  Rather, they are provided to compensate for shortcomings in private capital flows.  Some writers on development do not believe the shortcomings are serious enough to warrant aid interventions.[3]  One taking this position would argue that, at least on grounds of economic efficiency, private capital is going where it should.  Ostensibly, this would mean that private capital was moving to where it yielded the highest possible economic return.  There are two powerful arguments that can be made to counter this claim.  The first is that the world economy does not operate as a free market would.  Instead, all sorts of restrictions impair the free flow of inputs and goods. Therefore, there is no basis to believe that eliminating development assistance would move the world closer to an efficiency optimum.

Bauer and other critics of aid have pointed to uses of development assistance that have actually slowed the development process.  In a debate, one might counter these examples by pointing to excessive investments of the commercial banks in Latin America during the 'seventies. But that would only be a point to register in a debating contest.  In fact, and this is the second point, there is little basis to generalize that development assistance has worsened the allocation of world resources relative to the allocation that would have existed in the absence of such interventions.  One can say, however, that injecting development assistance into an economy that is giving inappropriate market signals to producers and/or consumers is likely to worsen rather than improve the situation.  In such circumstances, aid monies might be used either to leverage policy changes or to cushion their effects, i.e., to facilitate policy changes.

If one believes that development assistance has some role to play in increasing global well-being, the question then becomes how this aid should be allocated among developing nations.

It is simple-minded but useful to think of developing countries in take-off or pretake-off stages.[4] In the latter group, the conditions for take-off do not exist, i.e., there is not a sufficient pool of private resources to support the level of investment needed to propel the country forward onto a positive and sustainable development path. In the former countries, the needed private resources are available, while in the latter, they are not. This conception offers an argument for focusing aid monies in countries that are not yet prepared for take-off. The problem of identifying which countries are in the take-off stage remains, as does the question of whether or not the condition is reversible because, for example, of excessive debt service build-up or commodity price fluctuations.

But even if one could justify limiting aid to countries in the pretake-off stage, one must determine how much should go to each country. For example, one might address this question using investment criteria by asking how much aid and how much time will it take to get countries to the take-off stage. Using this standard some countries will look better than others. Perhaps the countries that do not look good by this measure should be excluded from "development" assistance and only qualify for relief and rehabilitation assistance. One does not have to pursue these musings very far before recognizing that economic reasoning does not offer a definitive answer to the question of what countries should receive aid.

The public finance literature offers another possible basis for allocating aid among developing countries. In all OECD nations, the central governments distribute funds to local areas, either directly or through lower-level governmental units. There has been extensive theoretical writing on what formulas should be used[5], but in most instances, aid monies are allocated by formulas that include population and per capita income.[6]

It is relevant to ask whether size of country might serve as a partial criterion for aid allocations. This is of immediate policy interest in light of the relatively small amounts of aid going to India and China. Putting the question more directly, does the large size of both countries justify their relatively small aid allocations? Assume aid is to be restricted to countries that are unable to obtain sufficient private capital to move them into the take-off stage. The research on direct foreign investment suggests that the large size of both countries' domestic markets should make them quite attractive to foreign investors. More specifically, studies indicate that the dominant reason for transnationals to invest in a developing country is to enter its market without having to pay various sorts of import duties.[7] Analyses of transnationals have identified a second and growing reason for their investment in developing countries: to take advantage of low-cost labor and produce for export.

For both reasons, i.e., "tariff-hopping" and produce for export, the transnationals should be interested in investing significant amounts in both India and China. Until recently, this has not happened, most likely because of restrictions against foreign private investment imposed by both countries. Nevertheless, the potential for significant private capital inflows exists in both countries. Indeed, there are few developing countries that look so promising for private investors as China and India. In these circumstances, it can be argued that the level of foreign aid monies going to these countries should not be increased until they make serious efforts to attract foreign private investment since foreign aid should serve as the residual rather than primary source of foreign investment for developing nations.

At this point, it worth trying to sum up and decide how one comes out on this important allocation question. It would appear reasonable that the greatest share of aid monies should go to the least well-off segment of Third World countries, and that the size of a country's population influence this share. Regarding the latter point, standardization by population allows one to highlight cases of abnormally low and high aid levels. Per capita income can and has served as a qualifier for some types of official aid. While one can argue about the per capita income level at which countries should no longer be eligible for ODA, there is, nevertheless, considerable appeal to the idea of establishing a graduation level: to the person who supports aid on humanitarian grounds, there is a level of affluence above which aid will not be warranted (with the exception of disasters); to the person who opposes foreign assistance on the grounds that it creates competitors and displaces workers in developed nations, the concern about aid is likely to increase as per capita income rises in the recipient nations. Large and serious pockets of poverty do exist in countries with high overall per capita income levels. Examples such as Brazil, Nigeria, and Thailand come immediately to mind. But one might legitimately ask whether it is the role of foreign assistance to deal with such internal inequalities. At the very least, a serious commitment on the part of the developing country to deal

with national income inequities would seem to be a
desirable precondition for external aid.

As stated above, a definitive case cannot be made for
how aid should be distributed. However, inasmuch as most
people would agree that there is a per capita income level
above which a country should no longer be eligible for
concessional financial assistance, some projections of
future aid levels to the year 2000 are presented below,
employing the $850 per capita income criterion to
distinguish between richer and poorer developing nations.
Very simple assumptions underlie these projections. The
first is that country per capita incomes will continue to
grow at the same rate as in the 1972-1982 period. Of
course, such an assumption cannot be defended: there is
little justification to assume the growth rates of the
last decade will continue. However, the exercise
presented below could be easily replicated using other
growth projections. A second assumption is that the
overall aid level will remain the same in real terms as it
was in 1982. The same criticisms can be made of this
assumption as were made of the first one.

The purpose of such an exercise is to address two
questions:

1. What would the savings be if aid were cut off
   to countries that were already above the $850
   level in 1982?

2. What would the savings be if aid were cut off
   to countries which moved above the $850 per
   capita income level during the 1982-2000
   period?

The answers are provided in table 5.3. The first
column presents total ODA by region in 1982. The second
indicates the amount of ODA going to countries with per
capita incomes less than $850 in that same year. The
third column indicates the amount of ODA going to
countries with per capita incomes less than $850 in 2000.

Table 5.3
Allocation of ODA Commitments and Savings
($ millions)

| Region | 1982 Total ODA | 1982 ODA to Poorer Nations | 2000 ODA to Poorer Nations | 1982 ODA Saving | 2000 ODA Saving |
|---|---|---|---|---|---|
| Africa South of Sahara | 7333 | 6240 | 5936 | 1093 | 304 |
| Middle East and Africa North of Sahara | 4733 | 1981 | 0 | 2752 | 1981 |
| South Asia | 4746 | 4746 | 4746 | 0 | 0 |
| Far East Asia | 2345 | 2153 | 524 | 192 | 1629 |
| Oceania | 868 | 339 | 473 | 529 | -134 |
| Central America & The Caribbean | 1882 | 504 | 807 | 1378 | -303 |
| South America | 1050 | 187 | 187 | 863 | 0 |
| TOTALS | 22957 | 16150 | 12673 | 6807 | 3477 |

Column four provides the answer to the first question raised above. If aid to countries that now have per capita incomes in excess of $850 were eliminated, an annual savings of $6.8 billion in ODA would result. Actually, the saving could be $7.6 billion because $802 million of official aid in 1982 went to Europe, a region omitted from this study.

Column five provides the answer to the second question. It indicates that there would be an annual savings of $3.5 billion if aid to all countries that moved above the $850 per capita level between 1982 and 2000 were terminated.

These savings could take the form of a reduction in ODA disbursements. Alternatively, they could be used to increase ODA disbursements to countries with per capita incomes lower than $850. At the extreme, if all the above-mentioned savings resulted in new disbursements to the poorer countries, their ODA levels could be increased by $11.2 billion, or 83 percent. There is a real question, given current development strategies and disbursement procedures, whether such a large increase would or could be effectively utilized. While it is unrealistic to expect that all aid to countries having per capita incomes above $850 will be terminated, $6.8 billion or roughly 30 percent of official disbursements in 1982 went to countries with incomes above $850. If that percentage were maintained in the year 2000, aid to poorer countries could be increased by $2.4 billion, or 15 percent.[8]

CONCLUSIONS

The above paragraphs indicate that the amount of official development assistance available to poorer nations depends as much on how these funds are distributed as it does on overall levels.  It is concluded that the OECD and other proponents of development assistance might consider adopting a new  goal that focuses on distribution.  Specifically, it is proposed that the goal should be to reduce the percent of ODA going to countries with per capita incomes in excess of $850 from 30 percent of the total to 10 percent of the total by the year 2000. It is recommended that this goal be adopted in addition to revising the guideline for ODA contributions by member states.

NOTES

[1]  Considerable analytical work has been done on the determinants of aid allocations.  For a recent imaginative effort, see Alfrad Maizels and Machiko K. Nissanke, "Motivations for Aid to Developing Countries," World Development, Vol. 12, no. 9 (1984) pp. 879-900.

[2]  Of course there are well-known problems with this definition of balance of payments circumstances and more sophisticated measures could be used.  The point here is strictly to portray an alternative measure.

[3]  For example, see P.T. Bauer, Equality, The Third World, and Economic Delusion (Cambridge: Harvard University Press, 1983).

[4]  W.W. Rostow, The Stages of Economic Growth (New York: Cambridge University Press, 1960).

[5]  See John W. Smith, "Principles of Grant Distribution Systems," OECD Urban Management Studies, Measuring Local Government Expenditure Needs: Copenhagen Workshop (Paris, 1981), pp. 251-280.

[6]  See Advisory Commission on Intergovernmental Relations, A Catalogue of Grant-in-Aid Programs to State and Local Governments (Washington D.C., 1984).

[7]  For a review of this literature, see Sean Nolan, "Transnational Enterprises and Manufactured Exports from

Industrialising Countries: Theoretical and Empirical
Significance," Yale University Department of Economics
Report (New Haven, 1983).
[8] Seventy percent of $3.477 billion.

# 6

## What Remains
## to Be Done

The last chapter projected per capita incomes for developing countries to the year 2000. Using these projections, however imperfect they may be, this chapter looks at countries that will still require development assistance in the year 2000. The point of doing this is that it provides a useful starting point for the consideration of future development needs.

REMAINING COUNTRIES

Consider first countries that are expected to have per capita incomes of less than $400 in 2000. These countries are presented in table 6.1, along with their projected populations. While the African continent will contain the largest number of countries (twenty-one) with per capita incomes under $400, Asia will remain the continent with the greatest number of poor people, even when China and India are excluded. Only Haiti among Central and South American nations will remain in this lower income category. If the 1982 official assistance levels were distributed among these regions, all the aid to Africa would go to poorer nations while in the other two areas, a large portion would go to better off nations, as table 6.2 indicates. Combining information from the

Table 6.1
Countries Projected to Have Per Capita Incomes Less Than $400
in 2000

| Africa | Population in 2000[a] | Asia | Population in 2000[a] | Cent. & So. America | Population in 2000[a] |
|--------|------|------|------|------|------|
| Ethiopia | 57 | China | 1196 | Haiti | 7 |
| Zaire | 55 | India | 994 | | |
| Tanzania | 36 | Bangladesh | 157 | | |
| Kenya | 40 | Pakistan | 140 | | |
| Mozambique | 24 | Vietnam | 88 | | |
| Uganda | 25 | Burma | 53 | | |
| Ghana | 24 | Afghanistan | 25 | | |
| Madagasca | 16 | Nepal | 24 | | |
| Malawi | 12 | Sri Lanka | 21 | | |
| Mali | 12 | Cambodia | 10 | | |
| Upper Volta | 10 | Laos | 6 | | |
| Guinea | 9 | Bhutan | 2 | | |
| Niger | 11 | | | | |
| Rwanda | 11 | | | | |
| Benin | 7 | | | | |
| Burundi | 7 | | | | |
| Somalia | 7 | | | | |
| Sierra Leone | 5 | | | | |
| Togo | 5 | | | | |
| C.A.E. | 4 | —— | | — | |
| TOTAL | 384 | | 2716 | | 7 |

Source: World Bank, World Development Report, 1984, table 1,
pp. 192-193.
[a] In millions.


Table 6.2
Distribution of 1982 ODA for Countries Projected to
Have Per Capita Incomes of Less Than $400 in 2000

| Area | $ millions | Percent of Total |
|------|------|------|
| Africa | 7,333 | 40 |
| —share to poorer nations | (7,333) | (100) |
| Asia | 7,959 | 44 |
| —share to poorer nations | (5,270) | (29) |
| Central & South America | 2,932 | 16 |
| —share to poorer nations | (128) | (1) |

above tables, it can be seen that poorer Asian countries
would receive only $2 per capita of official assistance,
while African and the Central and South American countries
would receive $19 and $18 per capita, respectively.

## Asia

Should a larger share of official economic assistance
go to Asian nations in the future, and if so, how should
it be used?  This is not an easy question to answer based
on any of the standard quantitative or humanitarian
measures development experts normally use to assess need.
Let's look at various clusters of countries in that part
of the world to begin to define the problem.  In chapter
5, it was argued that because of the size of their
domestic markets both China and India should get
relatively small amounts of foreign aid.  Neither country
has shown much interest in receiving the traditional forms
of technical assistance offered by the West: In India,
there is a large surplus of trained professionals; in
China, there is growing evidence the country can learn
from the West without importing large cadres of technical
assistance personnel.  And both countries appear to be
able to attract substantial amounts of foreign private
investments, if and when they want it.  Admittedly, this
will require policy changes to continue to attract and
keep foreign investors, but the opportunity is at least
there.  Nonetheless, policy makers, academics, and
development theorists in both China and India have
expressed interest in discussing economic development
problems with their counterparts in western nations.
Regarding other Asian recipients of foreign aid the
concerns of western donors should be different.  Take
Bangladesh, for instance, the country second only to Sri
Lanka among Asian nations as a recipient of aid on a per
capita basis.  In aggregate terms, growth in this nation
has been impressive, but many of the benefits have been
neutralized, it appears, by rapid population growth.  So
while the country offers a large market for private
foreign investors, and low-cost, semi-skilled and
unskilled labor, until progress is made in curbing
population growth rates, it is reasonable to question the
point in increasing development assistance.  Like
Bangladesh, Pakistan has shown impressive economic
advancement in recent years.  The country is in the
process of liberalizing its investment and trading

restrictions and this, coupled with its large urban
markets, should make it extremely attractive to private
investors.  But it too has failed to come to grips with
its swelling population.

For different reasons, the other projected remaining
poor countries of Asia do not offer much of an opportunity
for western foreign aid.  Vietnam and Burma are currently
following a central planning, socialist strategy that has
little in common with approaches promoted by western
nations.  While it is probably true that both countries
could attract considerable foreign capital, public and
private, if restrictions were relaxed, it is not at all
clear that this will happen in the immediate future.  In
the meantime, it probably makes sense to provide a small
amount of foreign assistance to encourage discussions on
public policies that favor the free market system.

Other Asian nations are experiencing political
turmoil, such as Afghanistan with the Russian occupation,
that make it extremely difficult from the perspective of
many western donors, to determine what a sensible
assistance program might be.  Cambodia and Laos have been
so devastated by wars that relief rather than development
assistance deserves the highest priority for some time to
come.  And Sri Lanka is regrettably entering into a period
of domestic strife that could bring to an end and even
reverse much of the incredible social and economic
development that has taken place there over the last two
decades.

Still other nations in the region, such as Nepal and
Bhutan, have awesome topography to challenge the creative
development expert.  In the case of Nepal, there has
probably been far more western assistance spent there than
economic prospects warrant.  Bhutan has similar
topographical problems to Nepal; it also has followed an
extremely centralized development strategy.

If any of these trends - mushrooming population,
political strife or war, antipathy to the free market
system - continue it will be difficult for western donors
to devise sensible, sustainable development assistance
programs attractive to their constituents and to the
recipients.  Furthermore, countries that are
geographically disadvantaged in some sense offer an
economic challenge that will become increasing difficult
to meet in the future highly competitive world.  In sum,
it seems that the creation of sensible development
strategies for all of these countries will take very
sophisticated thinking and considerable risk.  For the

most part, western economists are not currently qualified
to provide this form of assistance. There is little
question, however, that most of these countries would
greatly benefit from initiating meaningful population
control programs. Because of the large number of highly
skilled people in this region, many of the other forms of
needed technical assistance could be adequately and more
cheaply provided by neighboring Asian neighbors than by
western technicians.

## Middle East and The Caribbean

These projections indicate no country in either the
Middle East or the Caribbean will have per capita incomes
of less than $400 in the year 2000. On the other hand,
countries in both areas have received substantial sums of
foreign assistance for security or political reasons.
Without judging the political justification a nation might
have in giving so-called security assistance, there is a
fundamental incompatibility between attempting to purchase
political allegiance and trying to promote economic self-
sufficiency. No development strategy can be expected to
generate national self-sufficiency when the recipient
nation has been promised enormous amounts of economic and
military assistance. Such promises can easily overwhelm
any incentives the people might have to become self-
sufficient. Tragically, there is growing evidence to
support this assertion. The most notable cases include
Israel, Egypt, and Turkey, but many Caribbean nations are
well along in the process of becoming dependencies.
The problem is of particular concerned in the Middle
East. Egypt and Israel are receiving approximately $2 and
$3 billion annually in aid from the United States, and the
benefits resulting from these huge aid flows are not
readily apparent; peace is no closer in the Middle East
than prior to the initiation of large aid payments;
countries that were almost self-sufficient prior to this
largess are now experiencing unmanageable inflation and
balance of payments problems. If anything, if war breaks
out, it has the potential of being extremely destructive
because a considerable portion of the recent aid has been
used to purchase military equipment that could not have
been afforded without the assistance.

## Sub-Saharan Africa

People always start by saying one cannot generalize
about sub-Saharan Africa (SSA) - and then they generalize.

In fact, there are certain statements that are
generalizable. For example, granting there is some
validity to all the negative things that have been said
about SSA government policies, it also is true that much
of what has happened is attributable to worsening terms of
trade and the fact that the world economy did not rebound
from the second round of oil price increases in the same
manner as it did from the first.

Between 1970 and 1980 the terms of trade
deteriorated for low-income SSA nations by 11 percent and
have not recovered since then. As table 6.3 indicates,
the terms of trade for middle-income countries worsened on
average by 32 percent, but then recovered somewhat in the
1980-1984 period. The terms of trade improved
dramatically for oil exporters as a result of the two
rounds of oil price increases.

Table 6.3
Changes in Terms of Trade, Select African Countries

| Country/Group | % Change 1970-80 | % Change 1980-84 |
|---|---|---|
| **Low Income Oil Importing** | | |
| Ethiopia | -36 | 0 |
| Mali | -17 | 14 |
| Zaire | -49 | -14 |
| Burkina | -25 | 15 |
| Niger | -41 | -23 |
| Malawi | -28 | 27 |
| Tanzania | -7 | -6 |
| Uganda | 9 | -2 |
| Togo | 45 | -14 |
| Gambia | -30 | 37 |
| Somalia | -36 | 14 |
| Benin | -44 | 14 |
| Central African Rep. | 20 | -1 |
| Madagascar | -12 | 5 |
| Rwanda | 27 | -41 |
| Kenya | 1 | -6 |
| Sierra Leone | -31 | -5 |
| Sudan | 2 | -2 |
| Ghana | -4 | -43 |
| Senegal | -1 | -2 |
| Chad | 23 | 7 |
| Mozambique | -11 | 4 |
| average | -11 | -1 |
| **Middle Income Oil Importers** | | |
| Mauritania | -44 | -5 |
| Liberia | -47 | 2 |
| Zambia | -66 | -35 |
| Ivory Coast | 3 | 1 |
| Mauritius | -7 | -8 |
| average | -32 | -9 |
| **Middle Income Oil Exporters** | | |
| Nigeria | 426 | -6 |
| Cameroon | 4 | -18 |
| Congo | 488 | 4 |
| Gabon | 488 | 3 |
| Angola | 122 | 2 |
| average | 306 | -3 |

Source: World Bank, Financing Adjustment with Growth in Sub-Saharan Africa, 1986-90 (Washington, D.C., 1986).

In addition to the worsening terms of trade, government policy makers in sub-Saharan Africa assumed the 1979-1980 oil price increases would have an impact on the global economy similar to the 1973-1974 price increases: a sharp shock, a short slump, and a rapid recovery. They acted on this belief by entering into short-term debts expecting they could be liquidated as soon as the world economy rebounded. With hind-sight we know the global recovery did not occur until the mid-eighties, and commodity prices have yet to recover. It is somewhat unfair to criticize these government officials for failing to anticipate what would happen correctly.[1] Major donors were recommending policies based on similar assumptions.

This section presents our view of the long-term development prospects for sub-Saharan Africa and the role donors might play in support of these prospects. The immediate needs for debt rescheduling and other forms of required balance of payments support will be skipped as these issues are receiving adequate attention.[2] We make no claims for the correctness of our prescriptions beyond saying they are sufficiently reasonable to warrant a debate.

## Population Control

As a starting point, it is useful to define what can realistically be accomplished in sub-Saharan Africa over the next twenty-five years. A modest goal would be to raise living standards above the subsistence level so that droughts and other climatic changes can be met without massive amounts of foreign assistance. With this as the major objective, there can be little question that top priority should be given to reducing the population growth rate, a rate that is accelerating. Efforts to reduce population growth will not make an appreciable difference in terms of pressures on the land and employment needs over the next fifteen years. But beyond then, there is no action that will yield as high a return in social and economic development.[3] This is a strong statement, in light of the debate concerning the relationship between economic development and population growth.[4] However, the argument supporting an accelerated population growth rate presumes near-to full employment, and it is unimaginable that even its strongest supporters would argue anything approaching near-to full employment exists in SSA today.

During the 1965-1973 period, the population growth rate for in this region averaged 2.6 percent annually; that grew to 2.9 percent per annum between 1973-1983. The World Bank now estimates this rate will increase to 3.2 percent in the 1980-2000 period.[5] At this level the population will increase from 398 million in 1983 to 675 million in 2000. It is worth remembering a country with a 3.2 percent population growth rate will double every twenty-two years while one with a 2.0 percent growth rate takes thirty-five years to double. In sub-Saharan Africa only Mauritius is projected to have a population growth rate of less than 2 percent over the 1980-2000 period.

A comparison of this area with other parts of the
developing world on population issues is troubling: SSA
people want larger families and have higher fertility
rates as table 6.4 indicates.

Table 6.4
Family Size Preferences and Fertility Rates for a
Sample of Asian, Latin American, and SSA Countries[a]

| Country Group | Desired Family Size | Fertility Rate |
|---|---|---|
| SSA | 7.5 | 6.7 |
| Asia | 4.0 | 4.7 |
| Latin America | 4.3 | 4.7 |

Source: World Bank, Financing Adjustment with Growth
in Sub-Saharan Africa, 1986-90.
[a] These surveys were done between 1975-1983.

One generally acceptable analytical tool for
predicting fertility rates is the contraceptive prevalence
rate (CPR), the percentage of married women of
childbearing age using contraception.  In Asia the CPR is
around 50 percent; in SSA it is less than 5 percent.  The
World Bank estimates the contraceptive prevalence rate in
sub-Saharan Africa would have to increased to 25 percent
to reduce that population growth rate to 2 percent per
annum.

All the evidence suggests that without a major
initiative to reduce population growth rates sub-Saharan
Africa will inevitably become more dependent on outside
assistance for survival.  Donors recently agreed to make
the provision of aid conditional on economic policy
reforms: the reduction of government size and deficit;
increasing producer prices paid farmers; and, the adoption
of more realistic exchange rates and other policies to
promote private sector activities.  Given the pressing
need to reduce population growth rates and the acceptance
of using leverage to affect policy reforms, the provision
of additional development assistance to sub-Saharan Africa
should also be conditional upon the adoption of vigorous,
noncoercive population control programs in these
countries.

It is often claimed that population control involves
sensitive national political and cultural values, and that
donors should not push too hard on these issues.  We

suggest conditional requirements involving population
issues pressed by donors should have no greater political
impact than past stabilization programs required by the
International Monetary Fund have had.  The latter programs
often resulted in widespread unemployment and poverty that
generated serious political upheavals, yet they were
supported by donors and recipients alike.[6]  The point is
reforms in population control are more important than
further economic policy reforms.  If population growth is
not slowed, the benefits from the amounts of foreign aid
likely to be forthcoming will be more than neutralized.

## Widening Disparities Can Be Expected

     It is virtually certain that the differentials
between quality of life in SSA and all other developing
country groupings will continue to widen in the future.
Sub-Saharan Africa is simply too far behind in such things
as infrastructure, human resource development (including
entrepreneurial as well as technological capacities), and
institutional structures to imagine any other outcome.
Even when some progress is made in these areas, other
nations of the world will be progressing as well.
Further, it is unlikely these countries will have an
absolute advantage in producing anything significant in
the foreseeable future; costs are too high relative to
productive and marketing capacities.  Consider some
examples.  Relative to per capita income, government
workers get paid more than twice as much in SSA as in
Asia; the expenses of higher education are eight times
what they are in Asia and twice what they are in Latin
America; and the costs of agricultural researchers are
double the costs in Asia.[7]  While devaluations could
reduce these cost differentials, sufficient devaluations
are unlikely.

## Rethinking the Agriculture/Rural Development Focus

     For more than a decade donors have focused
development assistance on agriculture in rural areas.  For
several reasons, the theory and practice of this rural
focused development strategy needs to be reviewed.  A
major reason for this policy was to stem the flow of
migrants to cities.[8]  This did not happen: metropolitan
areas grew at the same annual rate of 6.1 percent between
1973-1983 as they did in the 1965-1973 period.  Moreover,
migrant laborers are not the major source of African urban

expansion inasmuch as they have only contributed 40
percent of the urban growth.[9]  Indeed, the very opposite
is more likely the case: effective rural development will
improve the linkages between urban and rural areas,
thereby making urban migration easier.  A recent survey of
development assistance concluded:

> In almost all cases, development activities in
> rural areas cannot be justified on the grounds
> that they slow rural-urban migrations....It
> appears that making changes in urban areas is the
> most promising approach to influencing rural-urban
> migrations.[10]

The justification for a rural-focused policy was
based in part on a belief that SSA could maintain its
share in international agricultural markets and use the
proceeds to finance national development.  It now appears
this is not true.  Agricultural production is cheaper in
many other countries; and because of massive world food
and other raw material surpluses, per unit prices are
likely to continue to fall.  As one expert has pointed
out:

> If all SSA economies were to raise coffee, tea,
> cocoa, tobacco and cotton exports 5 to 8% a year,
> the price elasticities and their combined share of
> world trade in these products are such that they
> would earn less, not more foreign exchange.
> Africa is not, in general, a low labour cost area;
> very few countries can mount labour-intensive,
> export zone type programmes with any prospect of
> success.[11]

Current research suggests that sub-Saharan African
nations can not easily regain past export markets.  It
therefore seems sensible that no investments, and this
includes agricultural research initiatives, should be made
that are based on this assumption until thorough marketing
studies have been done.  These studies should not be based
on the present situation, as is so often the case, but
should attempt to anticipate what is happening globally,
i.e., what new countries are entering commodity export
markets and what will be the reaction of current exporters
to a resurgence of competitive exports from sub-Saharan
Africa.

If the portfolios of donor-sponsored projects were
reviewed, it is probable that at least 30 percent of their

investments are based on the assumption that exports
markets would absorb increased production, resulting in a
net foreign exchange gain. Marketing studies of the sort
proposed above would probably show that this assumption
was rarely valid. These unjustifiable export-oriented
projects should be terminated, thereby freeing substantial
foreign and indigenous resources for other purposes.

## Food Self-Sufficiency

Food self-sufficiency is another matter. No nation,
particularly those with as little purchasing power as many
sub-Saharan African countries have, wants to rely on
imports for its food supply. Hence, it would seem
reasonable to promote food self-sufficiency as a goal for
most SSA nations. Table 6.5 gives a recent picture by
country of Sahelian dependence on food imports. Overall,
it appears that 19 percent of the food consumed comes from
imports. However, there are a number of countries that
have a far greater dependence on food imports. Botswana,
Mauritius, Cape Verde, Mauritania, Congo, and Sao Tome
import over 80 percent of their cereal needs. Given the
opportunity costs of foreign exchange, considerable
worldwide unemployment, and the absence of other
prospects, food self-sufficiency is a worthy goal for most
SSA countries to pursue. And it is possible that the
purchasing power so generated would be used to revitalize
rural areas and provide capital for the modern economy, as
was discussed in chapter 4.

Table 6.5
Cereal Production, Imports, and Consumption[a] in
Recent Years, Sub-Saharan Africa

| Country | Cereal Production Average 1980-84 | 1985 Production As Percent 1980-84 | Cereal Imports Average 1980-84 | 1980-84 Imports As Percent Consumption |
|---|---|---|---|---|
| Burundi | 396 | 100 | 21 | 5 |
| Comoros | 21 | 102 | 27 | 57 |
| Ethiopia | 5495 | 95 | 431 | 7 |
| Kenya | 2401 | 134 | 450 | 16 |
| Rwanda | 293 | 104 | 23 | 7 |
| Somalia | 382 | 156 | 346 | 48 |
| Sudan | 2637 | 173 | 700 | 21 |
| Tanzania | 3002 | 121 | 365 | 11 |
| Uganda | 1281 | 114 | 41 | 3 |
| Angola | 361 | 92 | 316 | 47 |
| Botswana | 28 | 71 | 154 | 85 |
| Lesotho | 148 | 112 | 159 | 52 |
| Madagascar | 2187 | 107 | 260 | 11 |
| Malawi | 1499 | 105 | 48 | 3 |
| Mauritius | 1 | 104 | 169 | 99 |
| Mozambique | 500 | 80 | 480 | 49 |
| Swaziland | 87 | 113 | 67 | 44 |
| Zambia | 942 | 112 | 247 | 21 |
| Zimbabwe | 2133 | 168 | 137 | 6 |
| Benin | 382 | 148 | 91 | 19 |
| Burkina | 1145 | 138 | 111 | 9 |
| Cape Verde | 4 | 23 | 64 | 94 |
| Chad | 437 | 158 | 95 | 18 |
| Gambia | 86 | 148 | 66 | 43 |
| Ghana | 623 | 116 | 195 | 24 |
| Guinea | 514 | 120 | 146 | 22 |
| Guinea Bissau | 118 | 157 | 43 | 27 |
| Ivory Coast | 927 | 122 | 544 | 37 |
| Liberia | 250 | 101 | 112 | 31 |
| Mali | 1140 | 123 | 205 | 15 |
| Mauritania | 43 | 186 | 210 | 83 |
| Niger | 1595 | 115 | 135 | 8 |
| Nigeria | 9256 | 125 | 2285 | 20 |
| Senegal | 714 | 174 | 599 | 46 |
| Sierra Leone | 578 | 97 | 112 | 16 |
| Togo | 318 | 113 | 71 | 18 |
| Cameroon | 925 | 113 | 226 | 20 |
| C.A.E. | 109 | 105 | 40 | 27 |
| Congo | 9 | 117 | 88 | 90 |
| Gabon | 11 | 107 | 40 | 78 |
| Sao Tome | 1 | 143 | 8 | 92 |
| Zaire | 960 | 121 | 313 | 25 |
| TOTAL | 44127 | 123 | 10295 | 19 |

Source: FAO, "Food Supply Situation and Crop Prospects in Sub-Saharan Africa, Special Report," (Rome, February 26, 1986).
[a] Production and import figures are in thousands of metric tons.

In pursuit of this goal, a primary responsibility of donors should be to monitor food aid distributions to insure they do not interfere with the incentives to produce locally. It would take another book to discuss producer incentives, but in this regard, it should be remembered that the large private voluntary organizations are paid well for shipping and distributing food aid. It can be expected that they, like the agribusinesses providing food aid, will resist efforts to cut back on food shipments.[12] Another responsibility of donors should be to identify the major bottlenecks to increasing food production. These will differ from one setting to another, but experienced development personnel can anticipate needs for various types of infrastructure investments and applied research. Donors should be prepared to support these activities, provided they can be justified solely on the basis of increasing food self-sufficiency.

A New Urban Focus

The development focus on rural areas in Africa has not slowed the rate of urban migration. African cities continue to grow, and the need for urban planning and infrastructure investments is becoming increasingly apparent. In the absence of obvious prospects for improving rural employment, attracting people to urban areas would at least have the advantage of making it simpler and cheaper to provide basic amenities.

But more positive arguments for an urban development focus can be made. It appears that the rate of education of people living in urban areas is more rapid than that of people living in rural areas, and family size preferences decrease. As has been indicated in chapter, 3, the major attraction to foreign investors of a country is size of market and associated marketing and distribution costs. At this point, cities in sub-Saharan Africa are not large enough to attract significant amounts of foreign investment. But they will be soon, and they will be far more attractive targets to foreign investors if they are well-planned and the appropriate infrastructure investments have been made.

It is not being argued here that donors should support urbanization in all countries of SSA. However, consideration should be given to creating four or five major urban agglomerations that would serve as centers of major industrial activity and transport modes for the

entire African continent. This is not a new concept.
About twenty years ago urban planners proposed that
secondary urban areas would generate their own development
dynamic once they attained a certain size, provided other
conditions were met.[13]  In fact, the concept was right,
but the place was wrong.  Urban planners were unable to
find acceptable ways to introduce urban growth in
secondary urban centers, but established urban areas in
Latin America and Asia grew and became the centers of
industrial development, much as they did earlier in
western nations.  Based on urban growth patterns in other
developing countries, and the deterioration of the
traditional agricultural economic base, it would seem
appropriate to thoroughly analyze the social and economic
advantages of supporting urban development in sub-Saharan
Africa.

## Institutional Development

One of the clearest lessons coming out of the last
fifteen years of development assistance in sub-Saharan
Africa is that the institutional infrastructure does not
function with reasonable effectiveness in the world
economy.  Institutional infrastructure, in our context,
means human capital and sensible processes or ways of
doing things that incorporate national value systems.
Compared to Asia and Latin America, countries in sub-
Saharan Africa have a shortage of skilled manpower.  This
includes entrepreneurs, managers, engineers, economists,
and the other technicians needed to run complex economies
with a reasonable degree of efficiency in the twentieth
century.  They also have not had institutions strong
enough to resist the onslaught of large numbers of donors.
The result has been that the donors rather than the
governments of SSA countries have determined what should
be done.
Donors now recognize what happened and have begun to
coordinate their activities.  Joint donor-host country
meetings have been held to set common goals, eliminate
project redundancies and inconsistencies, and work for the
adoption of policies to attain the agreed-upon goals.  The
problem with this approach is that foreign aid donors are
now independent institutions with their own agendas and
most importantly their own institutional survival to
maintain.  They are project generation machines, so it is
questionable how effective these coordination efforts will
be.  Even if they are effective, the organization that

chairs the coordinating committee will most likely
determine the development strategy, and that will probably
be a donor organization.  As indicated earlier, the
donors' track record in selecting proper development
strategies is quite mediocre, and there is no reason to
think it will improve in this forum.

### The Need for a Change in Donor Attitudes

Is it a desirable state of affairs for SSA countries
to be effectively controlled by donor agencies whose past
development performance has been far from distinguished?
It is somewhat ironic that a major player in the
development game, the World Bank, would articulate as well
as any group could what the long-term development
philosophy should be:

> ...governments in Africa must be seen to have the
> prime responsibility for designing their
> adjustment and investment programs and for
> coordinating aid and other financial flows.
> Donors can assist in the task--but they should not
> undermine this responsibility by trying to
> negotiate their own favorite package of policy
> reforms or by promoting their own pet projects.
> To this end, the African countries must strengthen
> their core ministries....[14]

This is extremely unlikely to happen.  The Bank has
shown little interest in fostering the sort of activities
needed to attain these goals.  In fact, as a former senior
Bank official has noted:

> The analyses lying behind these [the Bank's
> economic] reports is almost always undertaken at
> Bank headquarters in Washington.  Few prior
> understandings are made with a government on what
> the major policy issues for study should be, and
> little, if any, attempt is made to internalize the
> analysis within government by undertaking the
> analysis as a joint responsibility.[15]

There is a need for a change in attitude as well as
process.  The former Bank official continues:

> The accusations that the Bank is arrogant; lacks
> humility; is insufficiently respectful of a

country's political leadership; fails to recognize
variations in behavior patterns in different
regions and countries of the world; is a
technocracy out of control; and other criticisms
are too widespread to be ignored.[16]

Of course, more is involved here than the attitude
and behavior of one donor. In recent years, there appears
to have been a polarization of viewpoints:

...there have tended to be dialogues of the deaf
and an excessive concentration on specific themes
wrenched out of the overall economic context.
This process has polarized positions, and, in
doing so, has reduced both the growth of factual
knowledge and the ability to devise operational
programmes.... The picture is a good deal more
complex than the hard-line advocates and opponents
of particular strategies and policies appear to
assume.[17]

The above position would appear to be correct when it
comes to economic policies. In contrast, the question of
the need for population control in sub-Saharan Africa is
simple and obvious. Making aid conditional upon the
adoption of aggressive population control programs need
not be presented in an irritating fashion. It can and
should be presented on a take-it or leave-it basis. The
only area requiring discussion will be on how to define an
aggressive, noncoercive population control program.
Coming back to economic issues, a major point of this
book is to illustrate their complexity and the continuing
inability to formulate the "right" policies. In such
circumstances, the following prescription would appear
most appropriate:

Because the situation in most SSA economies is
very serious, because past results suggest serious
errors in donor and recipient policies and
analysis, because the present context requires
policy changes and because specific programmes
must relate to actual national contexts (not
generalizations intended to apply to 30
countries), and because difficult policies require
genuine national understanding and backing if they
are to work - dialogue is critical. But it needs
to be clear that what is intended really is

dialogue, in which donors acknowledge that they too need to learn more in order to formulate sensible programmes for their own actions.[18]

## Creating Policy Making Capacity in SSA Governments

As a result of the relationships between donors and SSA leaders, and given the time pressures under which national leaders operate, there is little prospect of increasing the capacity of the existing leader cadre to make more effective policy decisions. And yet, as one expert has noted:

> Effective...programmes require that the governments concerned view them as "their own". Imposed programmes are of dubious productivity.[19]

A number of nations in sub-Saharan Africa are presently unable to play this role. They could be assisted in obtaining outside advisors to allow them to play this role. But if such assistance is to work, the national leaders must be assured that the advisors are working for them and have a professional allegiance to the best interests of their country. There are, on the other hand, a number of SSA countries that will not want to assume such a leadership role. It is easier to respond to donors' demands than establish one's own lists of priorities. Besides, it is convenient to have donors to blame for unpopular policy measures. The real hope for both types of countries is their next generation. For those who assume professional posts, sound technical training will be adequate. But the leaders will require more. In addition to analytic training, they must also develop a new philosophic perspective that provides them with a new policy orientation. It is in the interest of western nations for their institutions of higher learning to play at least a partial role in the formulation of the philosophic perspective (and here we are talking about liberal arts institutions rather than land grant institutions).

Part of this training should focus on the international economic situation and in particular, the international organizations that these leaders will have to work with. The training should allow them to see the strengths and weaknesses of the donor organizations so that they will be able to deal with them in a manner befitting a group of traveling salesmen. Putting it somewhat less abrasively, developing countries will continue to bargain with donors on a variety of matters for the foreseeable future. A better understanding of the primary aims of the donors, their strengths and shortcomings, and the restrictions under which they operate could facilitate the bargaining so that all involved are made better off.

Providing funds for such training should be primarily a bilateral donor responsibility. Whereas they might engage in an active competition to attract students, the multilateral agencies would find it politically difficult to select institutions for funding from among its member countries.


NOTES


[1] This has been noted elsewhere: "They (sub-Saharan African government officials) read the OECD, IMF, IBRD studies of the day which predicted exactly that and prepared their responses accordingly." Reginald H. Green with Mike Faber, "Why Have Sub-Saharan Africa's Economies Fared So Badly in the Recession?" (Sussex: Institute of Development Studies, The University of Sessex, March 1984).

[2] See, World bank, Financing Adjustment with Growth in Sub-Saharan Africa, 1986-90 (Washington, D.C., 1986).

[3] S. Enke, "The Economics of Government Payments to Limit Population," Economic Development and Cultural Change, Vol. 8, no. 4 (July 1960), pp. 339-348.

[4] For a summary of the debate, see Benjamin Higgins, Economic Development (New York: W.W. Norton, 1968), chapter 29.

[5] Ibid., table 25, p. 92.

[6] For example, see Joan M. Nelson, "The Political Economy of Stabilization: Commitment, Capacity, and Public Response," World Development, Vol. 12, no. 10 (October 1984), pp. 983-1006.

[7] World Bank, Financing Adjustment and Growth, pp. 21, 30, 31.

[8] For a recent review of some of the issues involved, see Michael P. Todaro, "Internal Migration and Urban Employment: Comment," and William E. Cole and Richard D. Saunders, "Reply," American Economic Review, Vol. 76, no. 3 (June 1986), pp. 566-572.

[9] Richard E. Rhoda, "Development Activities and Rural-

Urban Migration: Is It Possible to Keep Them Down on the Farm?" U.S. Agency for International Development, Office of Urban Development Paper (Washington, D.C., 1979).
10   Rhoda, "Development Activities and Rural-Urban Migration."
11   Green with Faber, "Why Have Sub-Saharan Africa's Economies Fared So Badly," p. 9.
12   Indeed, the troubling behavior of private voluntary agencies in providing refugee assistance recently in the Sudan raises serious questions about whether their relative independence from review and supervision should be continued.  For documentation of this problem, see Barbara Harrell-Bond, Imposing Aid (Oxford: Oxford University Press, forthcoming).
13   For a review of this thinking, see Lloyd Rodwin, "Regional Planning in Less Developed Countries: A Retrospective View of the Literature and Experience," International Regional Science Review, Vol. 3, no. 2 (1978); see also J. Friedmann and C. Weaver, Territory and Function: The Evolution of Regional Planning (London: Edward Arnold, 1979).
14   World Bank, Financing Adjustment with Growth, p. 45.
15   Stanley Please, The Hobbled Giant: Essays on the World Bank (Boulder: Westview Press, 1984), p. 98.
16   Ibid., p. 99.
17   Green with Faber, "Why Have Sub-Saharan Africa's Economies Fared So Badly," p. 1.
18   Ibid., p. 14.
19   Gerald K. Helleiner, Statement prepared for the Subcommittee on Africa, Committee on Foreign Affairs, U.S. House of Representatives, Washington, D.C., February 23, 1984.

# 7

## Some Future Possibilities

A major theme of this book is that change will continue. Some of the changes can be easily anticipated, while others are more uncertain. For both types, it is useful to develop future scenarios and their policy implications. In passing, it is worth noting that few bureaucracies are enlightened and/or confident enough to support such exercises: their primary role is to pursue objectives established in the past.

The unemployment scenario (plausible but far from certain) presented in chapter 4 is an example of the type of exercise that is needed. In a similar spirit, several predictions are offered in this chapter. To emphasize the element of uncertainty, the predictions will be presented as hypotheses.

HYPOTHESIS ONE: In the past, aid donors have as often been wrong as right in their policy recommendations to developing countries; this trend is likely to continue.

### Evidence

A major aim of the 'seventies was to reduce income inequalities in developing countries by "targeting" aid to poorer members of society. Research suggested this could be done through projects covering specific rural areas that emphasized the participation of the poor in all aspects of project activities.[1] This approach did not work, in large part because donors overestimated their ability to alter income distributions by means of these project-specific activities. It also became quite apparent that attempting to involve the poor in donor-sponsored projects rarely worked because it was so contrary to customary forms of behavior.[2]  Hence, donors were fundamentally wrong in thinking they could significantly affect income distributions by methods employed in the 'seventies.  It remains to be seen whether the new approaches that focus on choice of industrial strategy and employment will be any more successful at reducing income inequalities.[3]

Donors were also clearly wrong in the 'seventies in failing to emphasize the importance of proper macroeconomic policies.  Today, they are attempting to correct this mistake through policy dialogue which is discussed below.  They also pursued a project-intensive mode of assistance in the 'seventies, and their inability to either coordinate or consolidate these activities led to confusion and the fragmentation of policy making in developing countries.  While most western donor agencies have recognized these mistakes and appear to be in the process of attempting to take corrective action, the question arises: Will their new initiatives be more sensible and fruitful than previous efforts?  To answer this question, two of the more popular "new truths" will be examined: policy dialogue and institutional development.

Policy Dialogue

Policy dialogue sounds like a sensible activity. And it would be if it involved a wide-ranging discussion of policy options taking place in a relaxed environment over a period of years between the West and developing countries.  To date, it has rarely been used that way.  Instead, it is better described as a process donors are using to force policy changes on developing countries.  Frequently, donors make their position more persuasive by conditioning aid payments on policy changes they want.  And again this is not a new strategy.

There are two fundamental problems with this form of policy dialogue.  First, it would be far better if developing country officials could be convinced of the desirability of the policy changes without being pressured into making them; indeed, the pressure may cause resentment and a rejection of the policy changes as a matter of principle rather than on the merits of their substantive strengths and weaknesses.  Second, there is reason to doubt the correctness of a number of the policy changes western donors are promoting.  While this is hardly surprising in light of the donors' track record in the 'seventies, it does warrant some elaboration. Several of the policy positions currently being promoted by donors are critiqued below.

## 1. Export Promotion

For the last decade, economists have debated the relative merits of import substitution and export promotion as major themes in a country's development strategy.[4] For the time being, proponents of export promotion appear to be winning the debate, and their philosophy is becoming a major tenet of World Bank policy. But the issue should not be which perspective is currently popular, for that is not of much use to developing country policy makers. Every country has industries it wants to promote and protect from outside competition, just as every country has some goods it hopes to export, for political reasons as much as economic considerations. From an economic standpoint, it probably makes sense for most countries to follow a policy that includes some import substitution and some export promotion.

Consider first the justification for promoting import substitution. The world is operating far below a full employment level. For most countries, this situation justifies some protected industries as a means to insure employment for people working in these industries. At a time when there is considerable world unemployment and high levels of export subsidies, the argument that a country should eliminate its trade barriers and follow the dictates of the market are not tenable.

We live in a world with high levels of direct and indirect export subsidies (remember OECD agricultural subsidies). Since most of the industrialized world subsidizes some exports, Third World nations feel justified in following similar policies. The tough question is what industries should be promoted for export. For many industries, current world prices are of little use in making this determination. For example, should Ghana try to refurbish its cocoa industry? In large part, the answer depends on what Nigeria and Brazil (two large cocoa exporters) would do in reaction to such an initiative.

Moreover, as was discussed in chapter 4, technologies are changing rapidly, and most markets are oligopolistic. Consider another concrete example: should a country get into the production of silicone chips, based upon current prices and costs? The answer is clearly no. Chip prices

continue to fall, and the market life for a particular
chip is only eighteen months.[5]
    So the answer to the question should donors support
export industries, is that such an approach might have
worked in the past, but it is too simple a solution to
work in the complex global setting today.  In most cases,
developing country interests will be best served by
policies that combine import substitution and export
promotion.

## 2. Increasing Producer Prices in Agriculture

    It has been well-documented that low producer prices
were a primary reason for the poor agricultural
performance in sub-Saharan Africa during the 'seventies.[6]
Consequently, getting African governments to increase the
prices paid to farmers has been a major element in the
policy dialogue.  As surpluses are now starting to appear
in certain crops in certain African countries, it it high
time to carefully review this theme.
    It is one thing to promote higher producer prices as
a means to achieve self-sufficiency in certain foodstuffs;
it is a quite different matter to promote it as a vehicle
to get African countries into world export markets.  While
such a strategy might seem appropriate at today's world
prices, there are good reasons to question the relevance
of these world prices as a reference point for a country's
future development strategy.
    In this instance, it would probably be more
appropriate to reverse the policy dialogue.  Leverage
should be used to get western nations to end the subsidies
they are paying their farmers which only add further to
world food surpluses.  Obviously, such leverage is
unlikely.  Global food needs should also be considered.
Will China and/or Russia soon end their need to import
large amounts of foodstuffs and what effect will this have
on world prices?  What are the production levels and
export plans of other major agricultural producers such as
Brazil, Canada, and Australia likely to be?
    The above points raise serious questions about
continuing to press sub-Saharan African countries to
increase producer prices.  At the very least, it is time
to carefully review this policy initiative.

## 3. Getting Prices Right

    This "slogan" is gaining popularity in donor circles.
In most cases, it involves eliminating price distortions

in domestic markets so that prices give the right signals
to the private sector. Given the large price distortions
that exist in many developing countries, it remains a
desirable long-term goal. However, there is a
transitional problem that has not gotten the attention it
deserves. Specifically, the elimination of price
distortions will rarely occur all at once; it is far more
reasonable to expect the distortions to be eliminated in a
piecemeal fashion. This opens the danger that during the
transitional period, even greater price distortions will
exist than is the case today, i.e., eliminating one
distortion might make another distortion even more
extreme.

## 4. Privatization

There is considerable evidence to suggest that
private firms operate more efficiently than government
entities in most areas of economic activity. There are,
however, exceptions. A primary reason for the Latin
American debt crisis (which now threatens to bankrupt a
number of large western banks) was the poor judgment of
many private banks in extending unsound loans. These
loans were made at a time the banks were looking to place
unprecedented amounts they received from oil-exporting
nations. The novelty of the situation does not excuse the
poor judgment: there was plenty of evidence at the time,
had the banks cared to consider it, that the countries
guaranteeing the loans would not be in a position to make
the debt-service payments due on them. The banks are now
desperately pressing for public bail-outs, and they will
probably get them.
Beyond private sector shortcomings, there are other
ways the private sector initiative could misfire. In many
developing countries, there are simply no buyers for
government parastatals that most agree should be converted
to private ownership. Putting it slightly differently,
the costs to government of making some of these entities
attractive to private entrepreneurs would exceed the
benefits of privatization. On this point, the experience
of England and France are relevant. Both governments
intended to sell a number of public entities, but found
that the private sector was only interested in purchasing
the profitable ones. If this was the experience in
countries with relatively large capital markets, one can
image the problems of trying to increase the role of the
private sector in nations with fewer profitable public
entities for sale and fewer buyers.

There are, naturally, other things that can be done to increase the role of the private sector. For example, steps can be taken to make public entities more effective. The main point is that every situation will be somewhat different and most will be quite complex, requiring skilled individuals to make them work. These experts are in short supply, and usually do not choose to work for foreign assistance agencies.

A review of policy dialogue initiatives to date indicates that donors have focused on short term goals with little view to the future scenarios suggested in this book. Donors have also been remiss in not providing developing countries with the expertise they need to effectively implement new policies. And finally, developing countries resent the western use of leverage to effect policy change. The goal should be to convince developing nations that the policy changes being recommended are in their own interest.

## Institutional Development

Institutional development has become almost as popular as policy dialogue in discussions about needed new initiatives among western donors. Much of this attention stems from an assessment of African assistance efforts over the last twenty years that concluded the institutional base on that continent was inadequate to take full advantage of the project-intensive type of development assistance being offered during that period.

Despite the popularity of this development thrust, no western donor has offered a comprehensive definition of institutional development and a program to bring it about. Instead, there has been an increase in the amount of technical training offered on such things as effective management practices, the use of computers, and privatization (some development experts define institutional development as increasing the role of the private sector). There has also been an effort made by donors to increase coordination among the various activities they sponsor. At least implicitly, the thinking behind this coordination effort is that recipient nations have neither the institutional capacity nor political clout to make their own determination of what they want from donors.

In light of the mistakes western donors have made, a major aim of any institutional development initiative should be to equip developing countries with the ability

to deal effectively with western donors.  This means
recipient nations should first determine what their
priority development assistance needs are.  Then, with
additional knowledge of donor programs and the strengths
and weaknesses of their institutions and capability to
work in different fields, they would select the best
qualified donor to fill their various assistance needs.
Certainly, they would make mistakes; but the mistakes
would be part of a longer-term institutional development
process.

HYPOTHESIS TWO:  There will be a dramatic reduction in the
demand for western technical assistance.

The general philosophy guiding the provision of
economic assistance is to help needy nations attain self-
sufficiency.  Funds, technical assistance, commodities,
and other resources are provided to initiate a dynamic
process of growth, with the assumption that these
concessional or quasi-concessional inputs will eventually
be unnecessary: recipient nations will gradually develop
an indigenous institutional and human resource base and
the capability to finance programs.
Technical assistance from one nation to another is a
large part of the development package, but it is not a
modern phenomenon.  Rather, it is the way it is provided
that is new.  When French engineers went to Russia in the
nineteenth century or German scientists emigrated to the
United States after World War II they left their homeland
to settle in a new country, to become part of a new
culture.  In contrast, western technical advisors who go
to Africa today go for a brief period, usually a couple of
years, to provide temporary help where there are shortages
of local manpower.  They rarely stay long enough to become
part of the decision making process, and they live as
privileged advisors far above the standards available to
most of their national counterparts, often causing
resentment and animosity.  However valuable their advice
might be, the current structure of most western technical
assistance programs mitigates against continuity and
equality of professionals.[7]
It is not easy to establish how much money donor
nations spend on technical assistance or, for that matter,
the magnitude of the technical advisory corps.  There are
individual technical advisors, volunteers, student
trainees, church members, employees of private voluntary
organizations, universities and consulting firms, and

staff of the innumerable bilateral and multilateral donor organizations. Information about technical cooperation (technical assistance and student trainees) provided by OECD countries is incomplete. Excluded are figures from the multilateral organizations and developing nations. What is available indicates that the number of experts and volunteers decreased from 90,457 in 1972 to 74,709 in 1982.[8] A significant reason for that decrease was the decolonization process, particularly in France and England. For example, the number of advisors from England to developing nations decreased from over 16,000 in 1972 to just 6,000 in 1982.

There are two reasons this decline should continue and encompass technical assistance provided by other western nations. First, the stock of trained nationals in all developing countries will increase steadily as large numbers return from training overseas. The challenge will be for developing countries to find effective uses for these personnel. Second, for those countries that still have manpower shortages there will be increasing opportunities to fill this need from trained individuals from other developing countries. The cost of technical assistance personnel from developing countries will be much less, and frequently, they will be better prepared to deal with the problems at hand than technicians from the West.

HYPOTHESIS THREE: It is in interest of western nations to initiate technical exchange programs to replace technical assistance activities in advanced developing countries that have "graduated" and no longer qualify for development aid.

Most donor organizations are required by charter to terminate aid once countries "graduate" into that nebulous part of the developing country hierarchy called advanced or emerging. To the extent that the ultimate objective of a bilateral or multilateral development agency is to put itself out of business as fewer and fewer clients need the product it peddles, this is sensible. But to the extent that development is considered an evolutionary process - a continuum of progress, reversals, and new momentum - this approach means the opportunity to explore mutually beneficial exchange programs between developed nations and advanced developing countries is lost.

The value of continuing programs has been recognized. Acknowledging the importance of these advancing countries for political reasons, for trade and investment, and for cultural and intellectual exchanges, the U.S. Agency for International Development recently prepared a strategy for advanced developing nations. The purpose of the program was to promote scientific and technical exchanges between public and private institutions in selected countries not currently receiving bilateral assistance. As the program was conceived the primary funding would come from participating private organizations in the U.S. and private and governmental institutions in the advanced developing nation. The agency's role would be as a facilitator only.[9]

The program, however, never started. Critics opposed it because it was considered in conflict with established economic relations between the U.S. and these newly advanced countries, that it would divert scarce resources away from the most needy nations, that it would cause bureaucratic jurisdictional problems, and ultimately be of marginal utility.[10]

Variations of this model have been tried by the U.S. and other western nations in different circumstances. The Swedish Commission for Technical Cooperation was established in 1976 to support feasibility studies, conduct training programs, and facilitate different types of cooperative programs between Sweden and middle-income developing countries. Since June 1974, the U.S. Saudi-Arabian Joint Commission on Economic Cooperation has been sponsoring programs in a broad range of fields. In the latter example, most activities under the aegis of the commission are even funded by the Saudis: the role of the U.S. has been to provide a "guarantee" of quality of technical teams carrying out the projects and to oversee the management.[11]

As more countries "graduate" from eligibility for concessional assistance, western nations should consider alternative organizational arrangements to maintain continuity in the development process. Advanced developing countries have the ability to determine their future; they have a corps of extremely well-qualified technicians to carry out programs. In many instances they have come up with better ideas for accomplishing development objectives than their western advisers have recommended. In a word, they have "graduated" from the status of a colonial nation receiving directed development programs.

The new relationships should be fundamentally different from those of the past. They should be based upon a philosophy of equality, mutual cooperation, and support.  Hence, it is probably inappropriate for them to be sponsored by western bilateral donor agencies.  A more suitable arrangement would be a technical exchange program between western nations and advanced developing countries. These exchanges could take many forms: one might be modeled on the Fulbright Program of visiting scholars; another might promote reciprocal cultural events; yet another might sponsor medical or other scientific exchanges.

It is in the interest of all nations that such exchanges take place.  Inter—country communications should not be left to the diplomats, the news media, and tourists.  Continuing the limited contact between developing countries and the West now provided by technical assistance and training provides some assurance that a solid base of mutual understanding and respect can be established and increased.


NOTES

1  For example, see Elliott R. Morss, John K. Hatch, Donald R. Mickelwait, and Charles F. Sweet, Strategies for Small Farmer Development (Boulder: Westview Press, 1976).
2  The Strategies for Small Farmer Development found participation in project activities was positively related to project success.  A review of the data base indicates that the only projects with high levels of participation were ones that were located in areas that had traditions of participation.  Hence, the evidence said nothing about whether donors could generate increased participation where it had not existed in the past.
3  For a statement of the new approach, see Gustav F. Papanek, Lectures on Development Strategy, Growth, Equity and the Political Process in Southern Asia (Islamabad: Pakistan Institute of Development Economics, 1986).
4  For example, see Vittorio Corbo, Anne O. Krueger, and Fernando Ossa, Export—Oriented Development Strategies (Boulder: Westview Press, 1986); and Jagdish N. Bhagwati, "Rethinking Trade Strategy," in John P. Lewis and Valeriana Kallab, (eds.) Development Strategies Reconsidered, chapter 3.
5  See David Wheeler and Ashoka Mody, "Automation and World Competition: Korea's Future in Semiconductors, Automobiles, and Textiles,"  Manuscript Boston University,

Center for Asian Development Studies (Boston, 1986).
[6] For example, see World Bank, Accelerated Development in Sub-Saharan Africa: An Agenda for Action, (Washington, D.C., 1981).
[7] David K. Leonard, "What is Rational When Rationality Isn't? Comments on the Administrative Proposals of the Berg Report," Rural Africana, Vol. 19-20 (Spring-Fall 1984), pp. 99-113.
[8] Information on technical cooperation and assistance presented in this and the following paragraphs came from various issues of OECD, Development Co-operation.
[9] U.S. Agency for International Development, "Strategy Statement for Advanced Development Countries: Draft," (Washington, D.C., April 24, 1984).
[10] Memorandum, Stephen P. Ferrar (Office of Management and Budget) to Richard Derham (PPC/Agency for International Development), August 28, 1984
[11] U.S. General Accounting Office, "Donor Approaches to Development Assistance: Implications for the United States," GAO ID-83-23 (Washington, D.C., May 1983), pp. 28-29; Interview, Bonnie Pounds, U.S. Director, U.S. Saudi-Arabian Joint Commission on Economic Cooperation, October 16, 1984.

# Index